That Patchwork Place®

Marie-Christine Flocard and Cosabeth Parriaud

PATCHWORK *Basics*

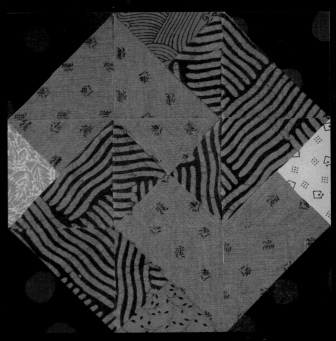

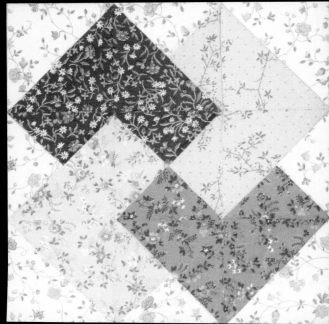

Credits

Editor-in-Chief
BARBARA WEILAND

Managing Editor
GREG SHARP

Design Director
JUDY PETRY

Text and Cover Designer
AMY SHAYNE

Design Assistant
CLAUDIA L'HEUREUX

Illustrator
BRIAN METZ

Illustration Assistant
LISA MCKENNEY

Copy Editor
TINA COOK

Proofreader
LESLIE PHILLIPS

Photographer
BRENT KANE

Translator
CHRISTINE LIGNEAU KOLSTOE

Acknowledgments

Our heartfelt thanks to:

Diane de Obaldia, owner of Le Rouvray, for her friendly help and encouragement;

Will Vidinic, for contributing five of the projects in this book;

Jacqueline Billion and the entire staff of Le Rouvray in Paris, for their enthusiastic support.

MISSION STATEMENT

WE ARE DEDICATED TO PROVIDING QUALITY PRODUCTS THAT ENCOURAGE CREATIVITY AND PROMOTE SELF-ESTEEM IN OUR CUSTOMERS AND OUR EMPLOYEES.

WE STRIVE TO MAKE A DIFFERENCE
IN THE LIVES WE TOUCH.

That Patchwork Place is an employee-owned, financially secure company.

Patchwork Basics
© 1995 by Marie-Christine Flocard
and Cosabeth Parriaud
That Patchwork Place, Inc.,
PO Box 118
Bothell, WA 98041-0118 USA

Library of Congress Cataloging-in-Publication Data
Flocard, Marie-Christine,
    Patchwork Basics / Marie-Christine Flocard
and Cosabeth Parriaud.
       p.   cm.
    ISBN 1-56477-085-0 (pbk.)
    1. Patchwork—Patterns. 2. Machine quilting.
3. Patchwork quilts. I. Parriaud, Cosabeth,
II. Title.
TT835.F55 1995
746.46—dc20   94-48046
                                          CIP
Printed in the United States of America
00 99 98 97 96 95   6 5 4 3 2 1

21.95

CONTENTS

Marie-Christine Flocard and Cosabeth Parriaud

Textile artists and quilting teachers for many years, Marie-Christine Flocard and Cosabeth Parriaud wrote this book at the urging of their French students, who asked for a book on the basics of machine and hand piecing a patchwork quilt. It is being published in both English and French.

Marie-Christine and Cosabeth offer their combined experience, advice, and special hints to help you make the projects featured in this, their second book on quiltmaking. Their first, *Le Rouvray,* written with co-author Diane de Obaldia, features quilts with a French flair from the teachers and staff of Le Rouvray, a popular Parisian quilt shop near Notre Dame.

Marie-Christine Flocard discovered patchwork in 1976 while she was living in the United States. She spent time there with her husband and family in the San Francisco Bay Area and in Boston. She took many quilting classes, several from renowned American quilter Roberta Horton. In 1989, after completing a career as a school teacher in France, Marie-Christine began teaching quiltmaking at Le Rouvray.

Marie-Christine has participated in many French and international quiltmaking expositions. As a member of the board of the French Quilting Association, she actively promotes international relations among quilters. In 1994 she organized "Patchworks and Fabrics of Jouy" in Jouy en Josas and has since developed a passion for this traditional French-made fabric.

Marie-Christine is married to Hubert Flocard, a nuclear physicist, and is the mother of two children, Cécile and François. They make their home outside Paris.

Cosabeth Parriaud studied at the Sorbonne in Paris, majoring in English. In the late 1970s she went to California and discovered the art of quiltmaking. It quickly became her passion and her vocation. She worked in a quilt shop in San Francisco for two years, and when she returned to Paris in 1980, Diane de Obaldia persuaded her to join the teaching staff at Le Rouvray. Cosabeth still teaches at the shop and manages the class schedules.

Cosabeth has designed quilts for other publications, including *Cent Idées, Elle-Décoration, Elle, Marie Claire Idées,* and *Madame Figaro* magazines. She has participated in a number of quilt expositions in France, other European countries, the United States, and Japan. She is especially well known for her colorful and contemporary designs.

Cosabeth is married and is the mother of two young boys.

WHAT IS A PATCHWORK QUILT?

Quilts are made of three layers of fabric: the quilt top, the batting or filler, and the backing. Making the quilt top is the creative challenge that awaits anyone who is intrigued and enticed by the designs and the stitching processes. Once the top is completed, it is layered with the batting and backing. Then the layers are joined with quilting stitches of a planned pattern, which add another dimension to the finished piece.

There are two basic ways to construct a quilt top (and many creative variations to explore once you have mastered the techniques of piecing and appliqué). Patchwork quilt tops generally consist of small pieces of fabric sewn together in geometric patterns. Appliqué quilts are made by cutting the desired shapes from fabric, then sewing them in place on a background fabric. The patchwork quilt is the subject of this book.

Fabric: "Sabine" by Canovas

QUILT ORIGINS

The origins of the patchwork quilt go back to antiquity. Tradition has it that the Crusaders brought back to Europe pieces of quilted clothing, copied after padded shirts worn by the Arabs of the Near East, to protect them from chafing and the cold. Europeans adapted the quilting technique for use with blankets. The production of these blankets was simple at first, but as the years went by the quilting became increasingly elaborate.

There are examples of quilting history throughout Europe. The treasury of the Chartres Cathedral includes a child's garment made of red linen quilted with horizontal lines, dated 1410. In the Netherlands, the oldest known patchwork is a doll bedspread (coverlet) dated 1680 and preserved in the Utrecht Museum. In England, a bedspread and tapestries from Levens Hall date from 1708. Quilt history is documented in writing as well. A memoir dating from the French Revolution mentions an appliqué quilt as a part of Queen Marie Antoinette's trousseau.

Whether they were sumptuous quilts or humble bedspreads, European quilts resembled each other in the general method of construction. The quilt top was a single piece of fabric attached to the other quilt layers with stitches. The European method of making these whole-cloth quilts crossed the ocean to the New World with the colonists.

In contrast to the whole-cloth quilts, American patchwork quilts were made of blocks, each containing two or more geometrically shaped pieces of fabric.

Inspiration for the block designs in historic quilts came from many places. Roman and Arabic designs inspired geometric motifs, such as the Baby block and Ninepatch. Other blocks, such as Wild Goose Chase and Ocean Waves, represent nature. Still others commemorate historic events and include Whig's Defeat and Rocky Road to Kansas. Jacob's Ladder and Star of Bethlehem get their names from biblical history.

A community tradition and social event, the quilting bee grew out of the necessity to turn quilt tops into quilts. At these gatherings, the completed top was stretched onto a large frame, along with the batting and backing. Then the participants added the quilting stitches, making short

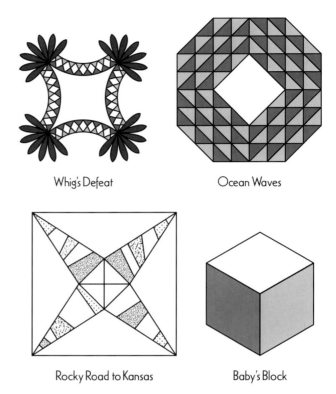

Whig's Defeat

Ocean Waves

Rocky Road to Kansas

Baby's Block

work of an otherwise time-consuming activity.

When a variety of inexpensive cotton fabrics became available during the Industrial Revolution, American women were able to make their quilts from fabrics purchased specifically for their decorative qualities.

The patchwork tradition in the United States experienced a revival in the 1930s due to the thrift required during the Depression years, then was all but abandoned after World War II. Lost but not forgotten, patchwork quilts were finally recognized in the late 1960s for their unique artistic qualities and as a part of the American heritage.

The first important exposition of antique quilts took place at the Whitney Museum in New York in 1971. In 1972 the exposition moved to the Musée des Arts Décoratifs in Paris, where it raised a great deal of interest and inspired numerous people in Europe to take up the art of the patchwork quilt. Today, quiltmaking is a thriving activity enjoyed by people around the world for its artistic content and is executed by those who love to create works of beauty and utility with stitches.

Getting Started

Before you choose a patchwork project, take a few minutes to familiarize yourself with the "Quiltmaking Basics" section of this book. If you are a new quiltmaker, you will find yourself referring to this section often as you assemble your blocks, sew them together, and finish your quilt.

Most of the quilts in this book are appropriate for beginners. Each project is marked with a symbol indicating its complexity. If you have never made a patchwork quilt before, we suggest you start with an easy project, indicated by a single patchwork block ▦. Once you have tried your hand at piecing, move on to a project marked with two blocks ▦ ▦ and then on to the more complex designs, indicated by three blocks ▦ ▦ ▦.

Choosing Quilting Materials
FABRIC

Always choose your fabric according to the use you have in mind for your quilt. If it's a bed cover, remember that the finished quilt will be handled daily and washed often. In this case, it is best to use 100% cotton fabrics of good quality. If you plan to use the finished piece as a wall hanging, the strength of the fabric is less important, and you can use fabrics other than cotton (silk, wool, and velvet, for example).

Preparation

Wash and iron cotton fabrics before cutting the pieces for your quilt. Since some fabric dyes bleed when wet, it is important to test all fabrics for colorfastness. Dark colors are particularly prone to bleeding. When fabrics bleed, they lose color in the wash water but do not always stain other fabrics in the same water. However, some do transfer to and permanently stain or discolor other fabrics.

To determine if your fabric is colorfast, put it into lukewarm (85°F) water. Rinse again if the water turns color. If the water turns color in the second rinse, make a white-vinegar solution with 1 quart of vinegar and 2 quarts of water. You need about 1 quart of this mixture for every yard of fabric. Add your fabric, allow to soak for half an hour, then rinse thoroughly. After prewashing and treating the fabric as described, allow it to dry until damp, then iron it on a piece of white fabric, such as muslin or another plain-weave cotton. If it still leaves a trace of color on the white fabric, you are taking a chance of further bleeding if you choose to use it.

Cotton fabric usually shrinks 1.5% to 2% in the first washing. Take this into account when purchasing fabrics. We allowed for this in the yardage requirements given for the quilt plans in this book.

After washing and pressing your fabric, straighten one edge by tearing across the fabric width. Then place it on a flat surface and fold it in half with selvages together. If you cannot align the torn and selvage edges without creating wrinkles in the folded edge, the fabric is off-grain. You can sometimes correct this by pulling fabric on the diagonal to stretch it.

Storage

There are many ways to store quiltmaking fabrics after washing and pressing them. Each quiltmaker finds a method that works for her. Marie-Christine stores hers in boxes or baskets. As you make more quilts and begin collecting fabrics, you may want to consider storing them on shelves like a collection of books as Cosabeth does. Grouping in color categories is helpful. If you can see your fabrics at a glance, it is easier to find just what you need. Do not store fabrics inside plastic; it traps moisture.

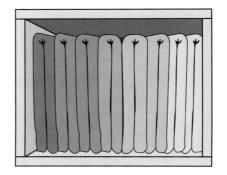

Width and Yardage Requirements

Fabric requirements for each quilt in this book are based on 44"-wide fabrics. We recommend that you preshrink all washable fabrics as described on page 7. Since cotton fabrics do tend to shrink, the yardage listed is based on a usable width of 42" after preshrinking. If your fabric is narrower, you may need extra. However, the yardage calculations are generous, so you should have leftovers of some of the fabrics to add to your scrap bag for future projects. We recommend cutting off the selvages. It is not wise to include them in your quiltmaking as their texture is stiffer and firmer than the remainder of the fabric.

COLLECTING FABRICS FOR PATCHWORK

When you choose fabric for your very first quilt, you will probably buy exactly what you need from a quilt shop. As you make more and more quilts, however, you may find it helpful to have your own collection of fabrics from which to choose.

Building a fabric collection is a good idea, so buy some solid-color fabrics and a variety of printed fabrics. Be sure to include fabrics from the various color families in a wide range of values (light to dark) and vary the intensity (brightness or dullness) too. Choose big prints, little ones, figurative designs, geometrics, and abstracts. Be sure to read "Color in Quilts" on pages 32–35 and look at the color combinations shown in the photos and in the color mockups.

We recommend buying no less than ¼ to ½ yard of any fabric you really like. For backing and borders, you need substantially more, so if you are buying ahead in anticipation of projects to come, 1 to 3 yards is safer. If you have graduated to planning and designing your own quilts, we suggest buying *at least* ¼ yard more than you think you need—just to be safe.

BATTING

There are several kinds of quilt batting from which to choose. Make sure that the batting you buy is washable. Avoid low-quality batting or batting designed for furniture. By the time you are ready to add the batting to your quilt top, you will have invested a considerable amount of time in the project. Don't skimp on quality.

If you are a new quilter, it is a good idea to sample several batting types and do a little quilting sample to see if you like the way the quilt layers (quilt top, batting, and backing) handle. For more information, see "Quilting Your Quilt" on pages 25–27.

Read the package directions. If the quilt you make from this book is your first, ask for assistance in making your batting selection at your local quilt shop. There are several different types from which to choose.

Cotton Batting

Cotton batting tolerates relatively high washing temperatures (104°F to 140°F). Cotton batting is nice to use when machine quilting because the cotton fibers grab the top and bottom layers of the quilt and keep them from shifting out of place. Cotton batting is non-allergenic, and the fibers do not migrate to the surface of the quilt top as they do in battings made of synthetic fibers. However, this type of batting is more difficult to quilt and sometimes shrinks in the wash. To keep cotton-batting fibers in place inside the completed quilt, you need to quilt more closely than when you use a batting made of polyester or a cotton/polyester blend. A needlepunched batting, such as Warm and Natural, requires less quilting.

Polyester Batting

Polyester batting is available in a variety of weights. Thinner batting is a good choice for wall hangings. Use a batting with more thickness or loft for bed quilts.

Other Batting Choices

Cotton/polyester blends, wool, and even silk are other batting choices. For flat, lightweight quilts, use a layer of thin cotton flannel, or for a heavier one, try a lightweight wool fabric.

Cutting the Pieces

Originally, patchwork quilts were made completely by hand. To cut the pieces for the blocks and borders, quiltmakers used patterns or templates and sharp scissors. They stitched the small fabric pieces together by hand. Traditional quiltmakers still prefer these methods, but many quiltmakers use speedier rotary-cutting and machine speed-piecing methods. Recognizing a need for both, we include directions for traditional methods and the speedier ones for each quilt when appropriate. Full-size templates are provided for all but the Log Cabin quilt on page 57, which does not require them. The pieces for most of the quilts featured in this book can be rotary cut if you prefer.

In general, when you create a patchwork block in the traditional manner, by hand or machine, you sew small pieces together to form bigger units, then join the units to create the block.

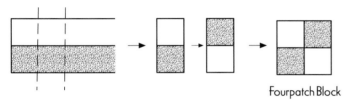

Fourpatch Block

For machine speed piecing, you sew strips together, cut the strips into segments, and then join the segments to create the blocks.

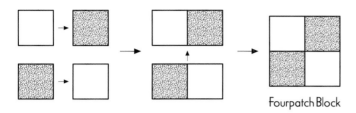

Fourpatch Block

The projects in this book are made of blocks, which in turn are made of several smaller pieces. Some quilt blocks, such as Jacob's Ladder, can be broken down into separate units.

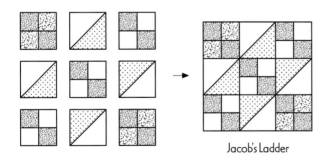

Jacob's Ladder

In order to cut the pieces for each block correctly, you first need to understand a little about woven-fabric anatomy. Fabric is made of two sets of yarns that look and feel more like fine thread. The threads that run lengthwise, parallel to the long finished edges called selvages, are the warp yarns. This is the lengthwise straight grain of the fabric. The threads that run across the width of the fabric (perpendicular to the selvages) are the weft or woof yarns—the crosswise straight grain. Those two directions are the most stable. Between the two is the bias grain. True bias lies across the intersections of the lengthwise and crosswise grain of a woven fabric. Warp (lengthwise

straight grain) and weft (crosswise straight grain) are equivalent when you cut small pieces for patchwork.

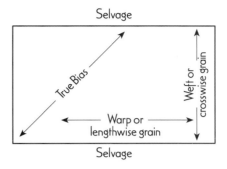

When cutting individual patchwork pieces, it is best to position the pieces on the fabric so that most of the edges are cut on the straight grain. Any edge that does not lie along a straight grain has some bias give and is therefore susceptible to stretching.

Study the illustration below and notice the grain line arrows. These indicate the straight grain. Imagine if these edges were cut on the bias. The edges of the block could stretch while you worked with the pieces and then with the completed blocks.

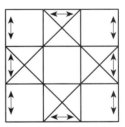

Each block template in this book has an arrow indicating the straight grain so you will know exactly how to cut the pieces for the best results.

Sometimes it is desirable to cut pieces with bias edges in order to use the design on the fabric in a particular way. For example, you may want stripes to run across a square on the diagonal rather than up and down. In this case, all four edges of the square are on the bias. You can do this as long as you are careful not to stretch the edges while you sew the block pieces together.

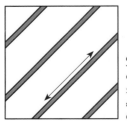

Stripes on the diagonal of a square All edges are on the bias.

For stability, sew these bias edges to other pieces that have straight-grain edges.

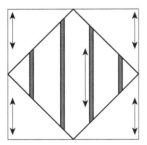

Read through the directions for the quilt you wish to make and decide whether you will cut with templates or use rotary-cutting techniques. You may want to use a combination of the two, cutting the block component pieces using templates and the border strips, sashing, and binding with rotary-cutting equipment. If you are unfamiliar with either of these methods, be sure to read "Template Cutting" below and "Rotary Cutting" on pages 12–15.

Before cutting any fabric, prepare it by preshrinking and pressing as discussed on page 7.

TEMPLATE CUTTING

If you prefer to use traditional quiltmaking methods, you need to make cutting templates for the pieces in your quilt. Use transparent template material available at your local quilt shop.

1. Trace the full-size template(s) from the pages of this book onto template plastic. Be sure to write the name of the quilt and the piece identifier (A, B, C, and so on) and mark the grain line arrow on the template. Carefully cut out the traced shapes, using paper-cutting scissors (not your good fabric scissors) or a rotary cutter reserved for this purpose.

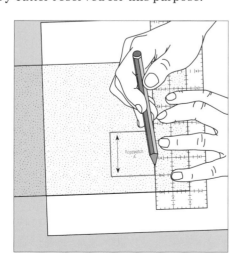

2. Position the templates on the wrong side of the preshrunk and pressed fabric and trace around the edges, using a sharp pencil. Since seam allowances are included in each template, you can butt them together as shown when cutting multiple pieces of the same unit from a single fabric.

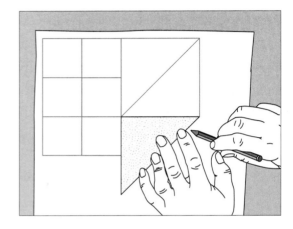

If the directions call for a reversed piece, for example, "Cut 1 Template B and 1 Template B reversed," turn the template over so the markings are backward and trace around the shape.

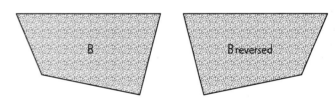

For light fabrics, use a hard HB pencil or a mechanical pencil. For darker fabrics, use a white, yellow, or #2 or #3 graphite pencil. Make sure the pencil is well sharpened so the lines you draw are fine and the template is as accurate as possible. Since fabric may slip as you draw, we recommend placing it on a sandpaper board; make your own by gluing sandpaper to a sturdy piece of cardboard. Glue small dots of sandpaper to the underside of the templates to keep them in place while you trace around them.

3. Carefully cut the pieces you have traced. Use a pair of scissors or a rotary cutter, ruler, and mat. See "Rotary Cutting" on pages 12–15.

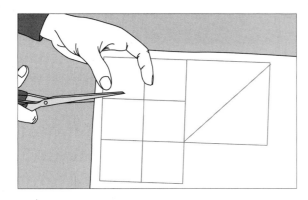

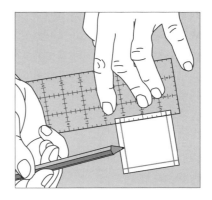

4. The standard seam allowance for patchwork is ¼"-wide. If you plan to piece by hand, use a sharp pencil and ruler and draw a seam line ¼" in from each cut edge as shown above right. Stitch on this line for accurate piecing.

If you plan to machine piece, eliminate marking the stitching lines *only if you can stitch an accurate ¼"-wide seam allowance.* Some sewing machines now have a special patchwork presser foot, designed so that the distance from the needle to the right edge of the foot is exactly ¼". You can also mark a stitching guide on your machine *exactly* ¼" from the needle on the bed of the sewing machine, using layers of masking tape.

MARKING AN ACCURATE ¼"-WIDE SEAM ALLOWANCE

Method One

1. Place a sheet of white paper on the bed of the sewing machine. Lower the presser foot, matching the edge of the foot with the outer right edge of the paper. Remove the top thread from the machine, then stitch a few inches.

2. Remove the sheet of paper and measure from the stitches to the edge of the paper.

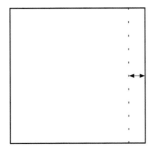

If the measurement is not exactly ¼", move the needle to the right or left (if you have a zigzag machine) and try the stitch test again. If you do not have a zigzag machine, or if you cannot adjust the needle position to obtain the desired stitch width, mark a stitching guide in the manner described below.

Method Two

1. On a sheet of white paper, draw a fine pencil line exactly ¼" from one edge. Use a very sharp pencil and be precise.

2. Place the sheet under the foot and let the needle down exactly on the line. Lower the presser foot. Place a piece of masking or colored tape against the edge of the paper, then raise the foot and needle and remove the paper. When

stitching pieces together, align the fabric edges with the inner edge of the tape for a perfect seam allowance.

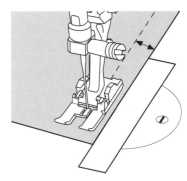

3. Test your new sewing guide on fabric scraps and measure the seam allowance after stitching to make sure it is accurate. Then add 2 or 3 more layers of tape to the first to build a slight ridge, which will make it even easier to guide the fabric edges for accurate stitching.

One of the advantages of template cutting is the transparency of the template plastic. Because you can see through it, you can position the template on the fabric to incorporate print motifs within the seam lines. Using templates is time consuming, however, and may not be as precise as rotary cutting.

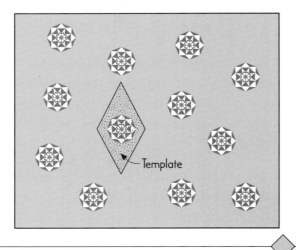

Template

ROTARY CUTTING

For rotary cutting, you need a rotary cutter with a sharp blade, a special rotary-cutting mat to protect the table, and a clear acrylic rotary ruler marked in accurate ¼" increments.

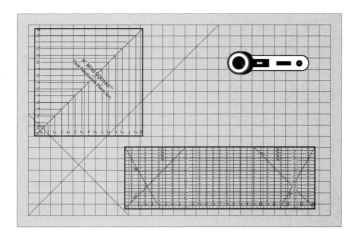

Once you have made the investment in these tools, you need only replace the cutting blade when it is dull. The ruler and mat will last a long time. If you are new to this technique, practice the following steps on scraps before cutting into the fabric for your quilt.

Cutting Strips, Squares, and Rectangles

1. Working on a rotary-cutting mat, fold the preshrunk fabric in half with selvages matching, then in half again so the first fold meets the selvage edges.

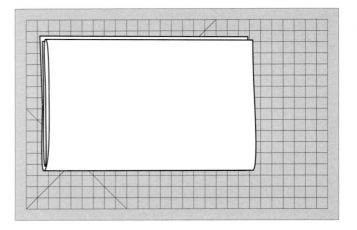

2. Position the ruler with one of the crosswise lines on the fold. Hold the ruler firmly in place, keeping your fingers out of the way of the cutter. If you are right-handed, the fabric will be to the right of the ruler as shown in the illustration below.

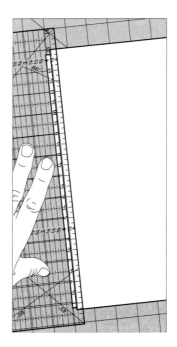

3. Bearing down on the cutter and moving it away from you right alongside the ruler, make a straight, clean cut through all layers.

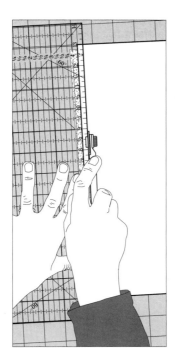

6. Crosscut the strips into the required squares or rectangles, using the appropriate line on the ruler.

If you prefer to use a smaller ruler to cut squares or rectangles from the strips, use the Bias Square®. For example, if you need 3" squares, cut strips 3" wide. Arrange a strip on the cutting board and place the Bias Square on top with one edge even with the top edge of the strip. Align the 3" lines on the Bias Square with the left and bottom edges of the strip; cut.

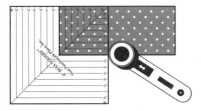

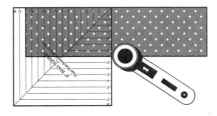

Glue a couple of patches of sandpaper to the underside of your ruler so it won't slip while you cut.

4. Lift the ruler and remove the strip you just cut.
5. Following the rotary-cutting directions for the quilt you are making, cut the required number of strips of the appropriate width. Line up the correct ruler line with the clean-cut edge of the fabric and cut.

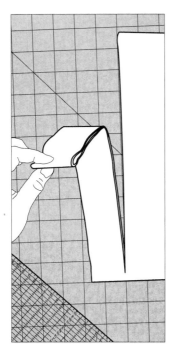

If the piece is a size that does not have a corresponding line on the square, cut an accurate paper template of the shape. Tape it to the Bias Square ruler and proceed as shown above.

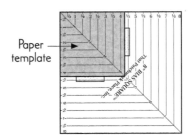

Paper template

Cutting Triangles

Many of the quilts in this book require triangles for the blocks themselves or for setting the blocks together. Templates are provided for these triangles; however, it is quite easy to rotary cut them.

Many block designs require half-square triangle units composed of two right-angle triangles. These are also called "bias squares." That's because the seam through the diagonal where the two triangles meet is on the bias.

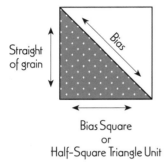

Bias Square
or
Half-Square Triangle Unit

Other designs, such as the popular Hourglass block, require quarter-square triangles. The long edges of the triangles are on the outside of this unit.

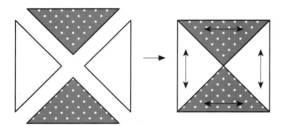

It is important to keep the straight grain on the outer edges of the units that make up a quilt block and the finished quilt. Use these triangle units in blocks and as side setting triangles in diagonally set quilts, where it is important to have the long edges of the quilt on the straight of grain to prevent stretching while the borders are added.

These two types of triangles common to quiltmaking require different cutting methods to position the straight grain correctly in each piece.

Cutting Half-Square Triangles

1. Cut a strip as indicated in the directions for the quilt you are making. Cut squares from the strip.

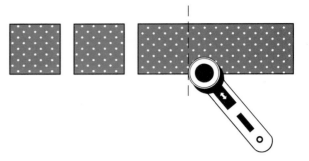

2. Using your rotary ruler or Bias Square cutting guide, cut the squares once diagonally to yield two right-angle triangles with the straight grain on the two short edges and the true bias on the long edge.

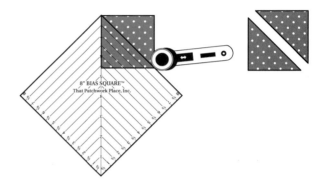

Cutting Quarter-Square Triangles

1. Complete step 1 above.
2. Cut squares twice diagonally to yield 4 triangles, each having the longest edge on the straight of grain.

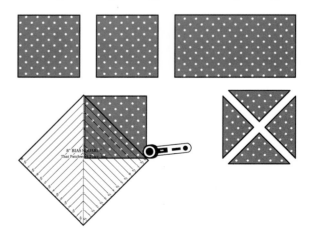

Although all required cutting dimensions are given with each of the quilt plans in this book, there may be times when you would like to rotary cut triangles for a quilt that does not have rotary-cutting directions. If so, use the following formulas to determine how wide to cut the strips that you will then cut into squares and finally into triangles.

To cut half-square triangles:

1. Determine the desired finished size *of the short side of the triangle. For example, you need half-square triangle units that finish to 3" on a side.*

2. Add $\frac{7}{8}$" *to the desired finished measurement determined in step 1 and cut strips this width. For 3" finished units, cut the strips $3\frac{7}{8}$" wide.*

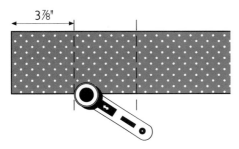

3. *Cut $3\frac{7}{8}$" squares from the strip. Stack the squares in groups of 4 and cut once diagonally.*

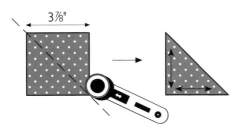

4. *Sew these triangles together in pairs along the bias edge. The resulting piece measures $3\frac{1}{2}$" square and finishes to 3".*

3½" (unfinished)

Half-Square Triangle Unit

To cut quarter-square triangles:

1. *Determine the desired finished size of the long side of the triangle. For example, you need an Hourglass block that finishes to 3".*

Hourglass Block
3" finished size

2. *Add $1\frac{1}{4}$" to the desired finished measurement determined in step 1 and cut a strip this width. For 3" finished units, cut the strip $4\frac{1}{4}$" wide.*

3. *Cut $4\frac{1}{4}$" squares from the strip. Stack the squares in groups of 4 and cut twice diagonally.*

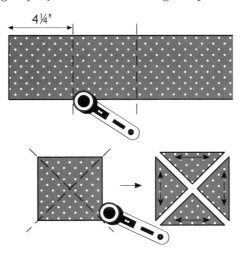

4. *Sew triangles of the required colors together in pairs and then sew the pairs together. The resulting piece measures $3\frac{1}{2}$" square and finishes to 3".*

N O T E
If you only need a few squares, rectangles, or triangles, use the Bias Square ruler to cut them quickly and accurately.

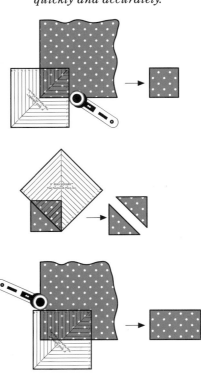

Sewing the Pieces Together

After you have cut your pieces following the directions in the quilt plan, decide whether you wish to hand or machine piece your quilt blocks. We give step-by-step directions for both techniques when appropriate.

HAND PIECING

Supplies

Thread. Choose a cotton thread for strong seams. It should match the dominant color of your fabrics. When joining fabrics of strongly contrasting colors, choose a thread to match the lighter of the two.

Pins. Use very fine, sharp pins.

Needles. Choose a fine, thin needle in a length that is comfortable for you to handle. Avoid needles that are too long or prone to breaking.

Thimble. Make sure it is comfortable.

Sewing Technique

To illustrate this lesson on hand piecing, we give step-by-step directions for making the block called Jacob's Ladder. (Directions for a cushion requiring this block begin on page 38. The illustrations that follow are for a right-handed person. Reverse them if you are left-handed.) To begin, lay out the pieces for the block you are making, referring to the block illustration and the color photo of the project.

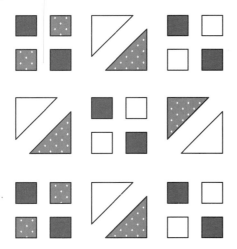

The following directions show you: how to sew squares together, how to join the finished units to make a four-patch unit, and how to join half-square triangles to create squares. You will also learn how to join the units within the block. Seam lines should be marked on the wrong side of each piece, as shown in step 4 on page 11.

To make a four-patch unit:

1. Place squares with right sides together and raw edges even. Pin at the seam intersection.

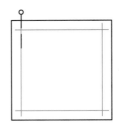

2. Thread the needle with a 12" to 18" length of thread. Make a simple small knot in one end, not a rolled knot, which tends to be too large and interferes with the piecing.

3. Insert the point of the needle in the unpinned seam intersection of the top piece. Guide it through the seam intersection on the bottom piece and bring the needle up to the top with a short straight stitch. Take a small back stitch, inserting the needle just before the knot at the seam intersection. This firmly anchors the beginning stitches, preventing them from coming undone later.

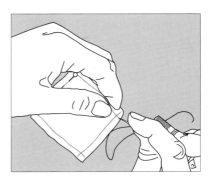

4. Continue stitching on the drawn seam line, taking small, straight stitches. Backstitch every fifth stitch.

5. To end the seam, take the last stitch slightly beyond the pin at the seam intersection. Leave the needle and thread on the back side of the work.

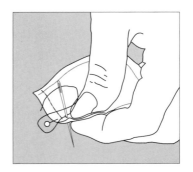

6. Turn the piece over and take 2 small, tight stitches, then one backstitch. Cut the thread, leaving a ¼"-long tail.

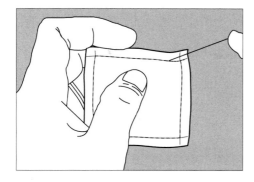

7. Follow steps 1–6 to make another two-square unit.
8. Place the completed units with right sides together and raw edges matching. Push the seams on the top and bottom to the left and insert a pin exactly at the seam intersection on the stitching line. Push the pin through the top layer, checking to make sure it is correctly positioned at the seam intersection. Continue through the second layer, again checking the seam intersections to make sure they match.

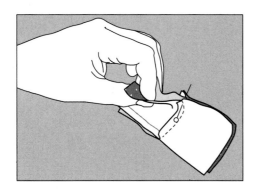

9. Add a second pin at the left end of the piece, inserting it through both seam intersections as you did when you joined the two squares (step 1, page 16).
10. Begin stitching as you did when joining squares. When you reach the seam intersection, remove the point of the pin so that it is in a vertical position through the intersection of the two seams. Insert the needle in the same hole where the pin is inserted, remove the pin, and make a backstitch that comes up on the same side of the seam intersection without catching either seam allowance in the stitch. Next, push the needle through the top seam allowance. Push the seam allowances to the right and take a short stitch without drawing the thread tight yet.

Open the seam to make sure the seam intersections match exactly.

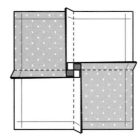

This   Not this

If the match is not perfect, remove the needle and reinsert it, pushing it slightly to the right or left as necessary until the top aligns with the bottom piece. Finish the seam as you did when joining the squares.

11. Press the seams, turning them in opposite directions as shown. Press first on the wrong side and then again on the right side of the completed unit.

To join two triangles:
1. Place 2 triangles with right sides together and raw edges matching. Insert a pin in the left-hand corner, piercing both layers of fabric at the seam intersection. This ensures accuracy. Add a pin in the center and 2 more along the long edge.
2. Sew the pieces together on the seam line; begin and end the stitching as directed in steps 2–6, beginning on page 16. Be careful not to stretch the seam as you stitch; remember, it is true bias. Press the seam toward the darker fabric.

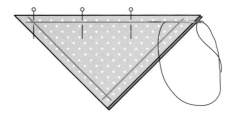

To join the block units and then the rows:

1. After completing all the required units for each block, arrange them in the correct block layout. You have 3 rows of 3 units each.

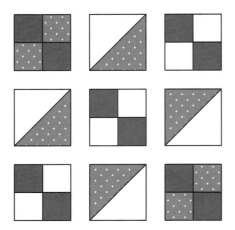

2. Sew the units together, using pins to secure the seam intersections as described in step 8 on page 17 (making a four-patch unit). When sewing a half-square triangle unit to a four-patch unit, begin stitching at the seam intersection in the half-square triangle unit.

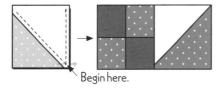

Begin here.

When reaching seam intersections, take care to use tight backstitches and do not catch the seam allowances in the stitching.
Before completing the block, check each row and unit carefully to make sure that the beginning and end of each seam is firmly anchored. If not, add a few stitches. Accuracy of the block relies on this.

3. Sew 2 rows of units together in the same manner, using pins to securely match the seam intersections where necessary. Place the first pin on the left. Place other pins at the intersections, keeping the seam allowances out of the way of the pins. Stitch. Remove pins and press.

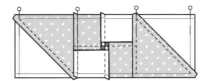

Add the remaining row of units to the edge of the center unit to complete the block. Press.

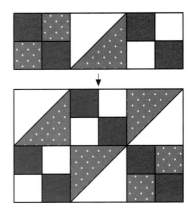

MACHINE PIECING

Supplies

Thread. We recommend either cotton or cotton/polyester thread. Choose a neutral tone, such as gray or tan. In the case of two highly contrasting colors, choose a neutral color or use bobbin thread that matches the lower layer in the unit you are piecing and a top thread that matches the upper-layer fabric.

Pins. Choose very fine pins.

Needles. Choose a fine sewing machine needle (size 70/10 or 80/12) and make sure it is sharp; a dull needle will damage your fabrics. Change the needle regularly.

Sewing Technique

Machine piecing is faster than hand piecing, but it requires precise stitching to ensure accurate ¼"-wide seams. As with hand piecing, you join pieces to make units, sew the units together to make block rows, and then sew the rows together to complete the block. There are a few differences, however, so be sure to read through the "Machine Piecing Tips" below.

Machine Piecing Tips

☐ Before you begin, adjust the sewing machine for a stitch length of twelve to fifteen stitches per inch.

☐ It is not necessary to mark the seam lines on the patchwork pieces if you know you can stitch an accurate ¼"-wide seam. See "Marking an Accurate ¼"-Wide Seam Allowance" on page 11.

☐ Insert pins perpendicular to the cut edge, always pinning first at any seam intersections or points that require matching as shown for "Hand Piecing" on page 16. Add pins at the beginning and end of each seam. Press seams in opposing directions as shown to avoid bulk at intersections.

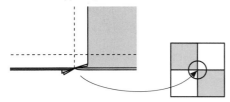

Press seams in opposing directions.

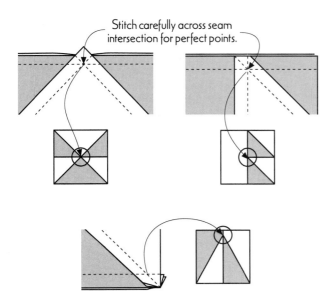

Stitch carefully across seam intersection for perfect points.

☐ If necessary, ease a slightly larger piece to fit a smaller one, so that the pieces and seam intersections match. Stitch with the slightly larger piece on the bottom. The feed dogs on the machine ease in the extra fullness as you stitch.

☐ Stitch from cut edge to cut edge, *exactly ¼" from the raw edges.*

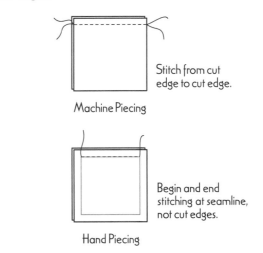

Stitch from cut edge to cut edge.

Machine Piecing

Begin and end stitching at seamline, not cut edges.

Hand Piecing

CHAIN PIECING

Use chain piecing to speed up your stitching and save thread.

1. Arrange the block pieces and pieced units on a work surface close to your machine.
2. Pin several pairs of units together for stitching.
3. Feed the first pair into the machine and stitch from raw edge to raw edge. Do not lift the presser foot.
4. Feed the next pair into the machine and continue stitching.
5. Repeat with any remaining pairs.
6. Remove the "chain" of pairs from the machine, clip the thread chains between them, and go to the ironing board to press the seams in the direction indicated in the quilt plan.

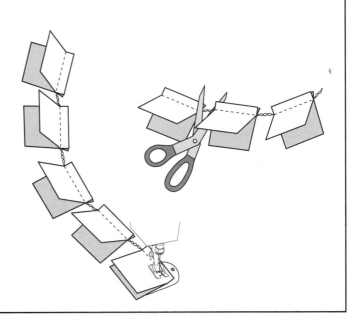

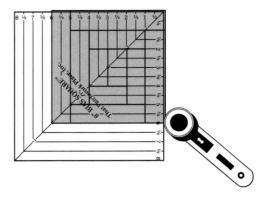

MACHINE SPEED PIECING

There are many patchwork units that can be assembled using a combination of strip cutting and machine piecing. The simple Ninepatch block is a good example. Instead of cutting numerous squares and then sewing them together, cut strips of the appropriate color and width, sew them together in a prescribed order, and then cut segments of the appropriate size and shape from the strip-pieced units.

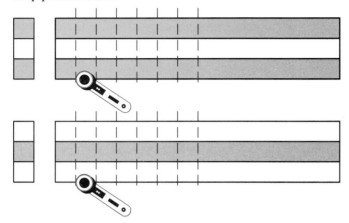

It is a simple matter to join the segments to create the required block units or the completed block.

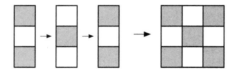

This is rotary cutting and strip piecing in its simplest form. It is possible to use these techniques to construct complex blocks. As you gain skill with these techniques, you may want to "graduate" to more complex methods. We recommend Shortcuts: A Concise Guide to Rotary Cutting *by Donna Thomas as an excellent resource for a variety of rotary-cutting methods.*

Assembling the Quilt Top

After creating the required number of patchwork blocks for your quilt, it is time to sew them together. Before you join the blocks, it is important to check their dimensions to make sure they are square and all the same size. Use the Bias Square ruler or a large square ruler and a rotary cutter to square up the blocks if necessary.

SETTING THE QUILT

Most of the quilts featured in this book are put together in a straight set. They are joined in vertical or horizontal rows, and then the rows are sewn together.

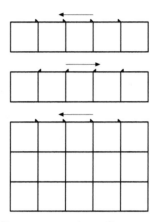

Press seams as indicated by arrows.

Some quilts require a diagonal set, where the pieces are arranged in diagonal rows and sewn together in the same manner, adding corners last.

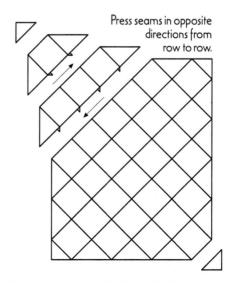

Press seams in opposite directions from row to row.

In either case, the quilt plan tells how to arrange and set the blocks for the easiest assembly.

In order to make it easy to join the completed rows so that seam intersections meet precisely, plan the pressing so that the seams between blocks are pressed in opposite directions from row to row as indicated by the arrows in the illustrations on page 20. Then pin and sew the rows together, placing pins at the seam intersections, just as you would if you were piecing block units together. See "Machine Piecing Tips" on pages 18–19.

ADDING BORDERS

Borders frame patchwork blocks and help stop the eye, drawing it back to the center of the finished piece. Some of the quilts in this book have no borders, while others have several. Borders may have straight-cut or mitered corners.

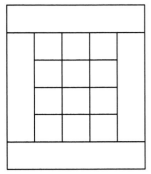
Straight-Cut Corners

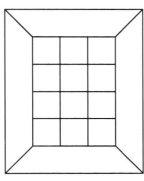
Mitered Corners

When adding borders to a quilt, it is essential to do so in such a way that you end up with a quilt with straight sides and square corners. Therefore, cutting directions for each of the quilts include the required number of border strips of the correct width, but you need to cut them to the appropriate lengths to fit your quilt top *after the blocks are joined*. How you do this depends on whether the quilt has straight-cut or mitered corners.

Borders with Straight-Cut Corners

1. Measure the length of the quilt top through the center and cut border strips to match that measurement. (In some cases it may be necessary to piece more than one strip together for a border of sufficient length.) Next, mark the centers of the quilt top and the border strips. With right sides together, pin the borders to the sides of the quilt top, matching the center marks and ends and easing as necessary. Sew the border strips in place. Press the seams toward the border.

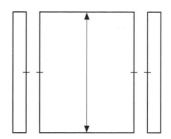

2. Measure the width of the quilt through the center, including the side borders just added. Cut border strips to that measurement, piecing as necessary. Mark the center of the quilt top and the border strips. Pin the borders to the top and bottom edges of the quilt top, matching the center marks and ends and easing as necessary. Stitch. Press the seams toward the border.

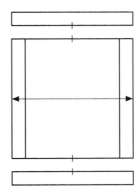

Borders with Mitered Corners

1. Estimate the finished outside dimensions of your quilt, including borders. Cut border strips to this length plus at least ½" for seam allowances; it's safer to add 2" to 3" to give yourself some leeway.

2. Mark the centers of the quilt edges and border strips. Pin the borders to the quilt top, matching centers. Stitch, using a ¼"-wide seam. The border strip should extend the same distance at each end of the quilt. Start and stop stitching ¼" from the corners of the quilt; press the seams toward the borders.

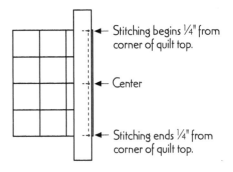
Stitching begins ¼" from corner of quilt top.
Center
Stitching ends ¼" from corner of quilt top.

3. Lay the first corner to be mitered on the ironing board. Fold under one strip at a 45° angle and adjust so seam lines match perfectly. Press and pin.

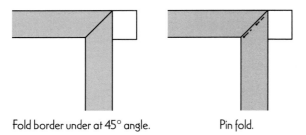

Fold border under at 45° angle.　　　Pin fold.

4. Remove the pins and carefully fold the quilt with right sides together, lining up the border edges. If necessary, use a ruler to draw a pencil line on the crease to make it more visible. Stitch on the pressed crease, sewing from the corner to the outside edge.

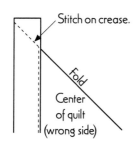

Stitch on crease.

Fold

Center
of quilt
(wrong side)

5. Press the seam open and trim away excess border strips, leaving a 1/4"-wide seam allowance.

6. Repeat with remaining corners.

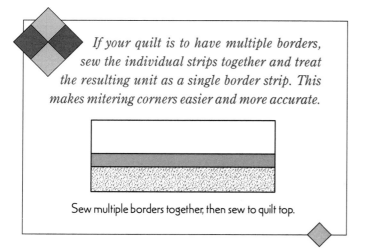

If your quilt is to have multiple borders, sew the individual strips together and treat the resulting unit as a single border strip. This makes mitering corners easier and more accurate.

Sew multiple borders together, then sew to quilt top.

Preparing to Quilt

You may quilt by hand or machine. Many modern quiltmakers prefer to piece blocks on the sewing machine, and then hand quilt the completed top. Others prefer the speed of machine quilting.

Quilting consists of stitched patterns that hold the quilt layers—quilt top, batting, and backing—together and at the same time add visual texture and interest to the completed quilt. It is much like adding raised drawings to the quilt surface. Old quilts are heavily quilted since only cotton batting was available and it required close stitching to hold it in place inside the quilt. The results of close quilting are truly beautiful. With the types of batting today, close quilting is not always necessary, but you may want to do it anyway for the lovely results.

Do remember that your quilt top will "shrink" a little in size as you quilt it. The stitches cause the quilt to draw up. The more heavily quilted it is, the more of this shrinkage occurs. This is especially important to remember if you make a quilt to fit a specific bed size.

MARKING THE QUILTING LINES

The directions for each quilt in this book contain information on how the quilt shown in the photograph was quilted. Quilt your quilt in the same manner or substitute another design of your choice. Some general advice that might help as you plan the quilting for your finished patchwork follows.

☐ We often accentuate geometric patchwork shapes by quilting 1/8" to 1/4" away from the seam lines.

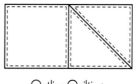

Outline Quilting

☐ Another way to enhance the geometric nature of the blocks is to quilt through the diagonals.

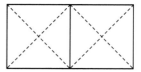

☐ Quilting in-the-ditch (in the seam line) is another easy alternative often used in machine quilting. The stitches are almost invisible once you learn how to guide the quilt to position the stitching in the seam line. If this is the only quilting you do, your quilt will have a puffier look than if you had used more elaborate quilting designs.

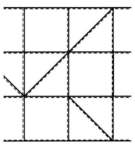

Quilting in-the-ditch

☐ Quilting patterns and templates for marking simple shapes and elaborate designs are available at your local quilt shop. Or, trace your own designs onto template plastic. Use a special double-blade cutter to cut slots along the design lines so you can trace the pattern onto your quilt top.

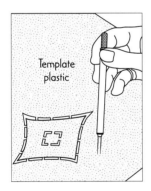

Template plastic

To test quilting designs on your finished patchwork before marking them, we suggest you draw a scale version of your quilt top on a piece of white paper. Then place a piece of tracing paper on top and draw in the proposed design, using dotted lines for the stitching.

Whether or not you need to mark the quilting designs on the quilt top depends on the type of quilting you do. Marking is not necessary if you plan to quilt in-the-ditch or outline quilt a uniform distance from seam lines. Mark more complex quilting designs on the quilt top *before* the quilt is layered with batting and backing. It is easier at this stage than after adding the other layers.

Choose a marking tool that will be visible on your fabric and test it on scraps to be sure you can easily remove the marks. Do not iron over marks made with these marking tools as heat may set them. Use masking tape to mark straight quilting. Tape only small sections at a time and remove the tape when you stop at the end of the day; otherwise the sticky residue may be difficult to remove from the fabric.

If you have created your own quilting pattern, there are several ways to transfer the quilting pattern to the quilt top.

☐ If the quilt top is light or medium in tone, trace the quilting pattern directly onto the right side of it. To do so, first trace the design onto paper using a black fine-tip marker. Place the quilt pattern on a light table or tape it to a window, lay the quilt on top and trace the lines.

☐ If the quilt top is a light color, trace the pattern onto tracing paper. On your work surface, place the quilt top on top of the batting and position the design as desired. Using a sharp pencil or a mechanical pencil, perforate the tracing at regular intervals. The pencil tip will leave small dots on the fabric for you to follow as you stitch. However, the design tracing will wear out; you need several copies to mark an entire quilt top of any size.

☐ Transfer the design to a piece of lightweight cardboard and use a thick, sharp needle to make perforations along the design lines. Then place the perforated cardboard on top of the quilt top and mark with a pencil through the holes.

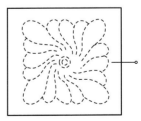

☐ Transfer simple shapes to a piece of template plastic and cut them out carefully. Lay the templates on the quilt top and trace around the outer edges.

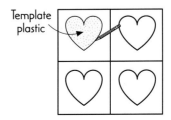

Template plastic

BACKING SELECTION AND PREPARATION

When choosing the backing for your quilt, select a fabric that is similar in weight and texture to that of the fabrics used in the quilt top. A fabric that is too firm and tightly woven is difficult to quilt. If you plan to wrap the edge of the backing onto the front of the quilt for a self binding as described on page 30, make sure the backing you choose coordinates with the colors in the quilt top. Don't forget to wash and iron the backing fabric before using it.

Unless the quilt is small and measures 40" wide or less, it is usually necessary to buy two or more quilt lengths of 44"-wide fabric for the backing. For the quilts in this book, cut the fabric into two equal lengths, then split one of them into two long pieces and sew them to the remaining length in one of the two configurations shown below. Press the seams open to make quilting through the layers easier.

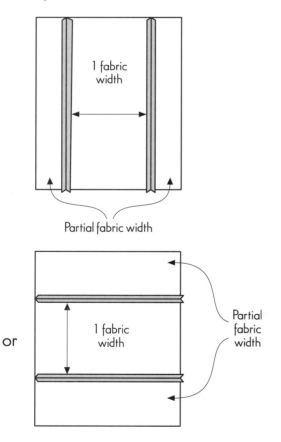

After sewing the strips together, trim the backing if necessary so that it extends 2" to 4" beyond the outer edges of the quilt top.

LAYERING THE QUILT

Unroll your batting and let it relax overnight before layering your quilt. Some batting types need to be prewashed, while others should definitely not be prewashed; be sure to check the manufacturer's instructions. Cut the batting to approximately the same size as the quilt backing.

If your quilt top is large, join two strips of batting to make a piece large enough. Simply butt the two edges and whipstitch together.

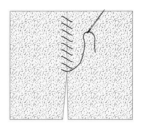

1. Spread the backing, wrong side up, on a flat, clean surface. Anchor it with pins or masking tape. Be careful not to stretch the backing out of shape.
2. Spread the batting over the backing, smoothing out any wrinkles.
3. Place the pressed quilt top on top of the batting. Smooth out wrinkles and make sure the edges of the quilt top are parallel to the edges of the backing.
4. Baste with needle and thread, starting in the center and working diagonally to each corner. Do not backstitch at the end of each row of basting. Instead leave a short thread tail. Continue basting in a grid of horizontal and vertical lines 6" to 8" apart.

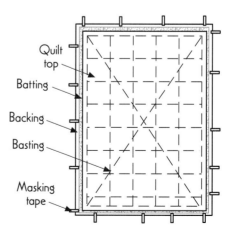

NOTE

If you plan to machine quilt, you may baste the layers with #2 rust-proof safety pins. Place pins about 6" to 8" apart, away from the area you intend to quilt.

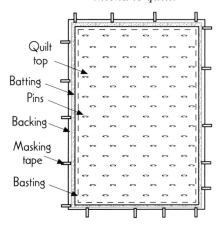

Quilt top
Batting
Pins
Backing
Masking tape
Basting

5. To prevent the batting from pulling away at the outside edges, remove the tape holding the backing to the work surface and fold the backing over the batting onto the quilt top. Baste in place with long stitches or use large safety pins.

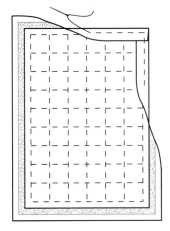

Fold excess backing over raw edges of quilt top and baste in place.

Quilting Your Quilt

Now it is time to add surface texture to your quilt top. Basic information on hand and machine quilting is included here. However, there are many fine references with more comprehensive information about each of these types of quilting. We suggest you add them to your quilt book library. For example, *Loving Stitches* by Jeana Kimball is a wonderful reference on hand quilting, and *Machine Quilting Made Easy* by Maurine Noble provides many lessons on this quilting format.

HAND QUILTING

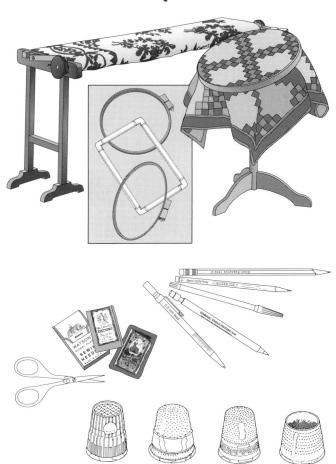

Supplies

Thread. Purchase thread made specifically for hand quilting. It is strong and lightly coated with wax to help it glide through the quilt layers. It is also less likely to knot than other sewing threads.

Needles. Use a short, size 10 or 12 Between needle. The shorter the needle, the tinier your stitches can be, but if you have never quilted, start with a slightly longer needle and graduate to the shorter ones later. The longer the needle, the more likely it will get bent and/or break.

Thimble. Even if you usually hand sew without a thimble, use one when quilting to help guide the needle through the quilt layers—and to protect your finger. Thimbles with flat tops, especially made for quilting, are available. To protect the finger that is underneath the quilt, use a plastic or leather finger protector. If you don't use one, a callous (very convenient) will develop after you have been hand quilting for awhile.

Frame or Hoop. Choose a round, oval, square, or rectangular hoop made of wood or plastic. The hoop holds the layers slightly taut to make stitching easier.

How to Hand Quilt

Begin by placing the center of your basted quilt layers in the hoop or frame and stretch the layers taut. Then put a little slack in the surface by tapping it with your hand. The quilt surface inside the frame should be flat but supple so that you can take several stitches at once.

1. Thread your needle with an 18" length of quilting thread and make a small knot at one end.

2. Insert the point of the needle into the quilt about ½" ahead of where you wish to start stitching. Pull it out at the starting point; gently tug to pop the knot through the quilt top to bury it in the batting. (Hide all beginning and ending knots in the batting in the same manner.)

3. To make the first stitch, place your needle perpendicular to the quilt top and move it through the quilt layers. Position your other hand under the quilt layers and use your index finger to tip the needle up and guide it back through the surface. The tipping motion is necessary to obtain regularly spaced stitches. You can use the pressure of your thumb to push down on the fabric so stitching is easier.

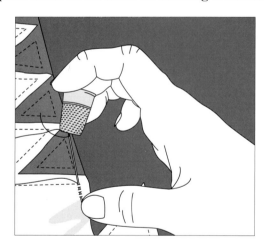

Remember, practice makes perfect! Fill the needle with several small stitches in a similar manner, then complete them by pulling the thread through all the layers.

4. Take a tiny backstitch to hide the thread in the batting. Clip the thread as close to the quilt surface as possible.

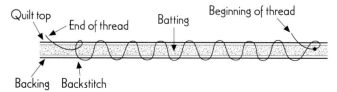

Quilt top
End of thread
Batting
Beginning of thread
Backing   Backstitch

For best results, remember the following rules:

☐ The needle must be perpendicular to the quilt top at the beginning of a run of stitches, then held at an angle as you fill the needle. It should never be parallel to the quilt top.

☐ Push the needle lightly through the layers, then block the needle point and guide it back up to the surface with the finger underneath. If you push it through too far, you will have to pull it back in order to make the stitch. You may then catch the stitch in the batting but miss the backing.

☐ Fill the needle with at least three stitches before completing the stitching motion, and use a thimble to help push the needle along.

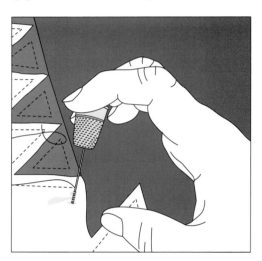

Your stitches may not be tiny at first; that comes with practice. Aim for an even length and even spacing between stitches at first.

☐ To move from one nearby quilting motif to another close one, slip the needle into the batting and pull it through to the point where you wish to begin on the next motif.

☐ Start quilting in the center of the piece, then move the hoop outward to unquilted areas in a symmetrical fashion.

☐ When you reach the outer edges of the quilt, baste strips of fabric to the quilt top so that you can still hold it in the hoop for quilting. Another way to extend the work for this purpose is to wrap 2"-wide strips of fabric over the frame as shown and use large safety pins to secure their ends to the quilt top.

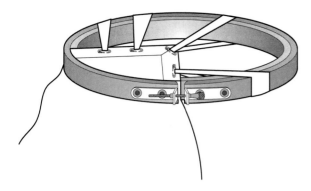

After completing the quilting, remove the work from the hoop and remove the quilting design marks and the basting. Then bind the quilt, using a method shown in "Binding" below right.

MACHINE QUILTING

Machine quilting is speedier than hand quilting and an alternative that many of today's quiltmakers are adopting and perfecting. The results can be quite breathtaking. The disadvantage of this method is that the continuous machine stitch results in a flatter finished appearance than does hand quilting. It is important to practice machine quilting on samples before you try it on your quilt.

Like hand quilting, unless you are stitching in-the-ditch of the seams, you need to mark the design on the surface of the quilt top before layering it with batting and backing. Baste by hand or use safety pins to hold the layers together as shown on pages 24–25.

Supplies

Thread. If you wish the stitches to be invisible, use cotton thread to match the backing in the bobbin and transparent polyester or nylon monofilament on the top of the machine. Use smoke-colored thread on quilts made of predominantly dark colors. Some quilters prefer to use cotton quilting thread on top rather than synthetic thread, but your stitches will be more obvious if you do. You may also use metallic threads to embellish your work.

Sewing-Machine Needles. Put a fresh, sharp needle in the machine before you begin.

Machine Quilting Tips

☐ Before you begin stitching, make a test sample by stitching through the selected backing, batting, and a sample block. Adjust the stitches so they are not too short. Adjust the tension so the stitching does not pucker.

☐ Begin and end stitching with a few tiny stitches so they automatically lock in place.

☐ If you are quilting in-the-ditch, use your hands to flatten and slightly pull the area on each side of the seam line to help guide the stitching so it doesn't "jump the ditch."

☐ If available, use the even-feed feature or a walking foot on your machine to avoid unsightly and undesirable puckers and pleats in the backing.

Finishing Your Quilt

When the quilting is complete, you are almost ready to spread your masterpiece on the bed or hang it on the wall. However, there is still a little finishing to do. First, you need to choose a binding treatment and add a hanging sleeve if you wish to hang your quilt. In addition, we recommend that you add an identifying label to your finished work.

BINDING

There are several ways to finish the edges of your quilt with binding. Three methods are shown here. Straight-grain and bias bindings may be attached to the quilt sides separately as shown in Method One, or they may be attached in a continuous strip as shown in Method Two. You may also use a self binding. This involves cutting the backing large enough so that you can fold it over to the front edge of the quilt.

The quilts in this book have single-layer straight-grain or bias bindings that finish to ¼" wide. Be sure to cut the binding strips on the bias for quilts with rounded edges or zigzag edges like those in the "Little Stars" quilt on page 106. Bias-cut binding is easier to handle on curves and corners since it has built in "give."

> *For quilts that will be used and laundered regularly, consider cutting 2¼"-wide binding strips. Fold the strips in half with wrong sides together and press. Attach to the quilt using Methods One or Two (pages 28–29). The double layer will wear longer than single-layer binding.*

Cutting Binding Strips

For Method One and Method Two, cut strips from your binding fabric in one of the following ways.

To cut single-layer, straight-grain binding strips:

Cut 1¼"-wide strips across the width of the fabric. You need enough strips to go around the perimeter of the quilt plus 10" for seams and the corners in a mitered fold. You may need to join strips to make them long enough to fit a side of the quilt top for Method One. For Method Two, join all strips into one long piece.

If you cut strips on the straight grain, join strips at right angles and stitch across the corner as shown. Trim excess fabric and press seams open.

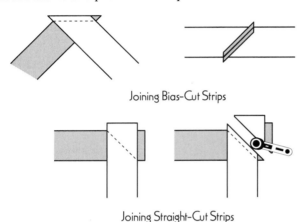

Joining Bias-Cut Strips

Joining Straight-Cut Strips

To cut bias binding strips:

1. Fold a 20" square of fabric on the diagonal. Press lightly, then cut on the fold. You can cut approximately 5½ yards of 1¼"-wide bias binding from this piece.

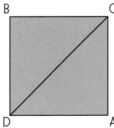

2. Sew the resulting triangles together as shown and press the seam open.

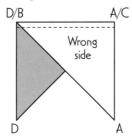

3. Draw parallel lines 1¼" apart on the wrong side of the fabric.

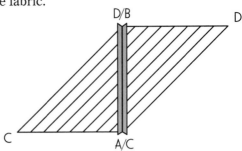

4. With right sides together and point C matching point D/B, pin the short ends of the piece together. Be careful to match the drawn lines to each other. Point A/C should extend beyond point D at the right-hand end of the piece. Stitch, then press the seam open.

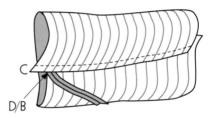

5. Cut on the marked lines to obtain a continuous strip of bias binding.

Adding Binding

Method One

1. Trim the batting and backing even with the quilt top edges.
2. Measure the length of the quilt through the center.
3. Cut 2 binding strips to match the quilt length.
4. Mark the center of each strip and the center of each long side of the quilt top.
5. With right sides together, centers matching, and the raw edge of the binding even with the raw edge of the quilt top, stitch a binding strip to each long edge of the quilt. Stitch ¼" from the edge.

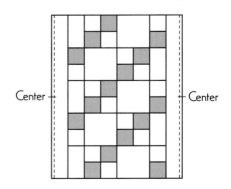

6. Turn the binding to the back side of the quilt, turning the raw edge under so the fold just covers the stitching line. Slipstitch in place.

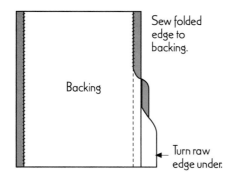

Sew folded edge to backing.

Backing

Turn raw edge under.

7. Measure the width of the quilt through the center and add 2".
8. Cut 2 binding strips to match this measurement.
9. Mark the center of the two short edges of the quilt and mark the center of each binding strip.
10. Stitch the binding strips to the short edges of the quilt top as described in step 5 above. One inch of binding will extend beyond the edge of the quilt at each end.

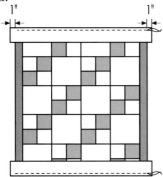

1"　　　　1"

11. Trim the excess binding to ½" at each end. Turn the binding to the back side of the quilt as described in step 6 above, folding the short ends in at the quilt edge. Slipstitch in place.

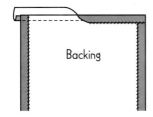

Backing

Method Two
1. Trim the batting and backing even with the quilt top edges.
2. Sew strips together as shown on page 28 to make one long strip of binding.

3. Turn one strip end under ¼" at a 45° angle and press. Turning the end under at an angle distributes the bulk so you won't have a lump where the two ends of the binding meet.

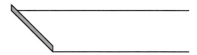

4. Starting on one side of the quilt and using a ¼"-wide seam, stitch the binding to the quilt, keeping the raw edges even with the quilt top edge. End the stitching ¼" from the corner of the quilt and backstitch. Clip the thread.

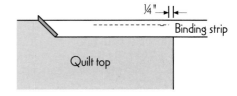

¼"　Binding strip

Quilt top

5. Turn the quilt so that you can stitch down the next side. Fold the binding up away from the quilt.

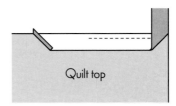

Quilt top

6. Fold the binding back down onto itself, parallel with the edge of the quilt top. Begin stitching at the edge, backstitching to secure.

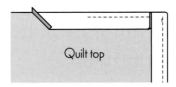

Quilt top

7. Repeat on the remaining edges and corners of the quilt. When you reach the beginning of the binding, overlap the beginning stitches by about 1" and cut away any excess binding, trimming the end at a 45° angle. Complete the stitching.

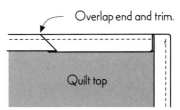

Overlap end and trim.

Quilt top

8. Fold the binding over the raw edges of the quilt to the back. Turn under the raw edge so the binding just covers the stitching and slipstitch in place. A miter will form at each corner. Slipstitch the mitered corners in place.

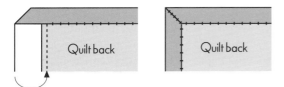

Self Binding

If you plan to wrap the backing to the front of the quilt to finish the edges, follow these easy steps.
1. Trim the batting even with the raw edges of the quilt top.
2. Baste ¼" from the cut edge, stitching through the quilt top, batting, and backing.

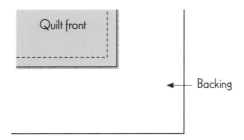

3. For a finished binding width of ¼", carefully trim the excess backing, leaving ½" of fabric extending beyond the outer edges of the quilt top.

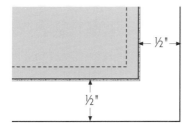

4. Fold each corner of the backing over the point of the quilt so the fold touches the corner of the quilt top.

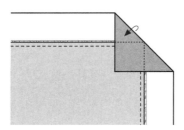

5. Fold the backing in so its raw edge meets the raw edge of the quilt top.

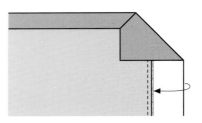

6. Fold again so the folded edges meet or just barely cover the stitching line; a miter will form. Pin in place.

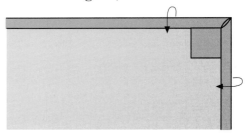

7. Trim away the small square of fabric that extends beyond the binding folds.

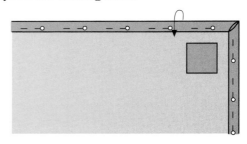

8. Slipstitch the binding in place.

ADDING A HANGING SLEEVE

If you plan to hang your completed quilt on the wall, add a hanging sleeve to the back to hold a dowel or curtain rod. When you make a sleeve following the directions below, the sleeve is the only thing that comes into direct contact with the hanging device (a wooden dowel or curtain rod). This is good quilt conservation.
1. Cut an 8"-wide strip of the backing fabric (or other coordinating fabric) that is 1" shorter than the top edge of the quilt.
2. Narrowly hem each short end of the strip.

3. Fold the strip in half lengthwise, wrong sides together and stitch ¼" from the raw edges. Press the seam open. Arrange the strip so the exposed seam is centered on the back side of the tube.

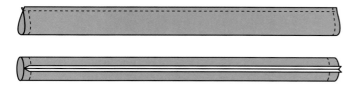

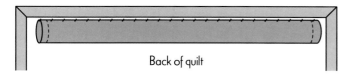

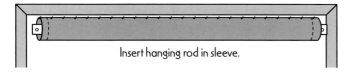

4. Pin the sleeve to the back of the quilt with the top edge just below the inner edge of the binding. Slipstitch the top, side, and bottom edges to the quilt backing, being careful that the stitches do not go through to the front of the quilt.

Back of quilt

5. Insert a dowel or curtain rod that is just shorter than the top edge of the quilt. The ends should extend slightly beyond the ends of the hanging sleeve.

Insert hanging rod in sleeve.

ADDING A LABEL

Don't forget to sign and date your quilt so that future generations will know its history. Consider embroidering your name and the date of completion somewhere on the front or back of the quilt. If you prefer, write or embroider pertinent information on a fabric label, then stitch it to the back of the quilt in one of the bottom corners. If you write the label, be sure to use a permanent-ink marker.

Caring for Your Quilt

If you use your quilt regularly on a bed, you will want to launder it occasionally. Choose a non-corrosive soap for hand as well as machine washing. Use cold or lukewarm water. If you decide to machine wash and dry your quilt, use a delicate drying cycle. Do not hang a wet quilt on a line to dry. The weight of the remaining water will cause fiber distortion and weakening. To avoid distortion, drape the quilt carefully over two dowels resting on the edges of the bathtub or on a drying rack.

If pressing is necessary, use a steam iron and a light hand to remove any wrinkles. Heavy-handed ironing flattens the loft of the quilt and stiffens the batting.

If you have many quilts, plan to rotate them, carefully storing the ones not in use to avoid set-in creases and light damage.

Storage Recommendations

Fold your quilt in thirds. If you store it for long periods, it is a good idea to place a piece of acid-free tissue paper inside the folds to help prevent sharp creases. Unfold and refold the quilt regularly to avoid creating permanent creases in the quilt. Store quilts in a pillowcase or in a clean sheet, not in a plastic bag.

We recommend folding your wall quilt first on a horizontal line, parallel to the top and bottom edges of the quilt. When you hang it, the weight of the quilt pulls gently on the horizontal folds, causing them to disappear faster than if you fold along the length of the quilt.

COLOR IN QUILTS

Color is perhaps the most important element in patchwork since it is what the eye perceives first. We all have a sense of color and we often behave in a subjective manner when choosing fabrics for a patchwork project. We choose fabrics in our favorite colors and eliminate others, thus restricting our quiltmaking palette.

The true joy of creating patchwork is feeling confident enough to experiment in order to compose your own designs. In this section devoted to color, we outline a few principles and give tips to guide you in selecting color for your quilts.

Identifying Color Families

Colors are divided into families in order to identify them more easily. They are usually represented on a color wheel like the one shown here. The twelve colors on the color wheel are called pure colors. Neither white nor black is shown on the wheel, but they are important colors to include in your work.

Primary colors. There are three primary colors: red, yellow, and blue. They are called primary since they do not contain any other color, and all the other colors are combinations of these.

Secondary colors. These are obtained by combining primary colors, and there are three of them: orange (red and yellow), purple (blue and red), and green (yellow and blue).

Tertiary colors. Combining primary and secondary colors creates tertiary colors. There are six of these: yellow-orange, red-orange, red-purple, blue-purple, blue-green, and green-yellow.

Neutral colors. These are important components in quiltmaking because they act as backdrops for the color families. Neutrals include all shades of black, white, off-white, beige, and gray.

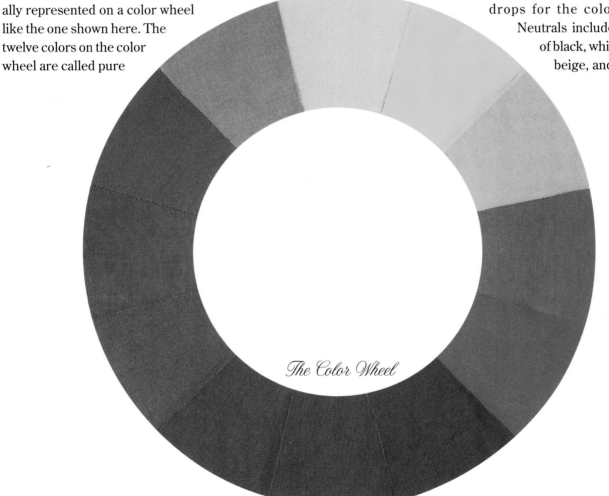

The Color Wheel

Understanding Color Characteristics

There are several ways to describe the qualities of any color. Understanding these characteristics and learning to consider them as you choose fabrics helps you achieve the desired effect.

VALUE

In color theory, value means the lightness or darkness of a color. It also indicates the amount of black or white that has been added to a color. In painting, adding white makes lighter values; adding black makes darker values. Pink is a light value of the color red, for example, and burgundy is a dark value. Peach and rust are light and dark values of orange, respectively. The light or dark nature of a color is relative and varies when positioned next to other colors. A medium shade may seem dark if positioned next to fabrics of light value. However, the same medium shade will appear light if positioned next to a fabric of dark value. This notion of relativity of values enlarges the characteristics of each fabric. It is a very versatile tool in quilt design and planning.

INTENSITY

In theory, this indicates the degree of saturation of a color. In painting, it is possible to modify the intensity of colors. By adding gray to blue, we obtain a blue-gray that is not a different color than the blue but a different intensity of it. A blue next to a blue-gray brings out a contrast called contrast of saturation. Intense colors stand out more to the eye than dull colors.

The twelve colors of the chromatic circle can be changed in a variety of ways depending on whether the intensity or the value is adjusted. Remember that each of your fabrics relates to one of the twelve colors in the circle unless they fall into the category of neutral colors.

COLOR COMPLEMENTS

Each of the twelve colors on the color wheel has a complementary color. A pair of complementary colors always contains the three primary colors. The six pairs are: yellow and purple, red and green, blue and orange, yellow-orange and blue-purple, red-orange and blue-green, and red-purple and green-yellow.

On the wheel, the complementary pairs are directly opposite each other. When you mix complementary colors, you change the intensity and you obtain grayed tones. If you look at a group of gray fabrics, you will notice that some really do have chroma or color—a red-gray or a yellow-gray for example.

COLOR TEMPERATURE

Colors are often defined as warm or cool. The warm colors on the color wheel are yellow, yellow-orange, orange, red-orange, and red. Cool colors include purple, purple-blue, blue, blue-green, and green. Technically, yellow-green is a cool color and red-purple is warm. However, color temperature is relative. Some red-purples appear warmer than others. The same is true of yellow-greens. The warm or cool character of a color also varies depending on the positioning of the color. For instance, a purple looks cold when positioned next to red or orange. On the contrary, the same purple looks warm when positioned next to blue or green.

Warm colors stand out or advance more than cool colors, which tend to recede. Think about using this color characteristic to make sections of a quilt design stand out or act as background.

COLOR CONTRAST

Color contrast is a fundamental concept in patchwork designs. Without contrast, all the colors seem to melt into each other. With carefully planned arrangements, some colors seem to pop from the surface. In the photo at right, we used a range of blue fabrics, close in value. The resulting block is flat in appearance. The points and star center are almost indistinguishable against the other geometric shapes in the block.

There are several ways to create contrast in patchwork. Two of the most valuable are discussed below.

Value Contrast

A piece of advice often given to beginners starting their first patchwork piece is to choose three fabrics different in value: a light, a medium, and a dark. If the pattern requires a fourth value, the choice may be a light, two mediums, and a dark. The bottom right photo shows a block with light-medium-dark contrast in a monochromatic (single color) scheme. You can create the same kind of contrast using several colors. In the photos below right and at the top of page 35, notice how the star design changes with the value arrangement.

Complementary-Color Contrast

The contrast between two complementary colors intensifies them. Positioning two pure complementary colors next to each other creates a strong effect, often overbearing. Pure complements often seem to vibrate next to each other, which tends to tire the eyes. Uneven quantities—a large amount of one with smaller amounts of the other—creates the contrast needed to give depth to a quilt. Don't forget to use complements with different values and intensities, such as light/medium/dark values or bright and dull intensities.

The multitude of available prints offers numerous possibilities. For example, if you wish to create a patchwork in blue tones, add to your scale of blue fabrics a blue print containing little orange motifs and a rust print (a dark value of orange) as shown in the bottom photo on page 35. Even if at first you don't like orange, you will recognize that this addition, while discreet, enhances the block design and makes it more visually interesting.

Review the list of complementary colors, studying them on the color wheel. Keep them in mind as you undertake a fabric search for your patchwork project. Learning to use complementary-color contrast successfully is very rewarding.

A block done in close values of blue lacks sparkle and visual interest.

The same block in the same blue color family but with light and dark values is more interesting. Value interplay creates visual depth.

*Several colors in different values create an even
more interesting block design.*

*Rust complements shades of blue in this
complementary color scheme.*

Developing
Your Color Sense

Our students often complain that they don't have a good sense for color and that they have a hard time choosing their fabrics. However, you can study color and form your own color sense. Developing color consciousness is the key.

Before launching into a project, cut small pieces of fabric and make a collage. Repeat this by varying the arrangement of the colors and adding or removing some. The results will all be different and will provide you with multiple choices for the composition of a patchwork block. This is the most interesting part of the patchwork. Go ahead and try it out! Do not forget how important it is to play with all colors, even those that at first do not particularly appeal to you. You can never predict in advance how they will come out when arranged next to other colors. Experiment, enrich your vision, and increase your possibilities for creating interesting quilts.

There are block mockups, using a variety of color combinations, with most of the quilt projects in this book. As you examine each of these fabric collages, notice how different a single block design can look, simply by varying the fabric colors and their relationship to each other in the block.

Whatever you do as you explore the wonderful world of quiltmaking, don't let color intimidate you. It is the key to making every quilt you sew a visual treat and the process of constructing it rewarding and exciting.

JACOB'S LADDER CUSHION

*Jacob's Ladder Cushion
by Cosabeth Parriaud,
Paris, France, 1994.
16" x 16".
Pieced and quilted by hand.*

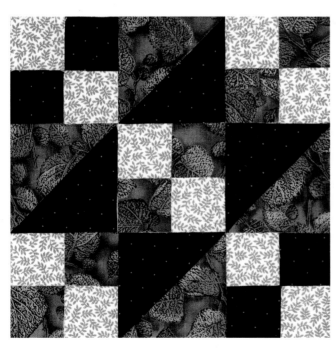

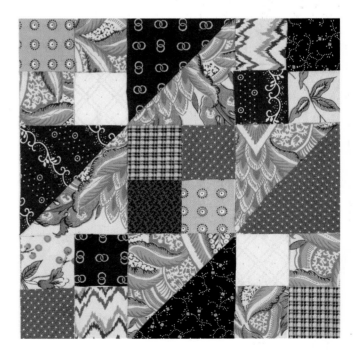

JACOB'S LADDER CUSHION

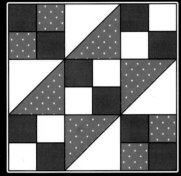

Jacob's Ladder Block

■ BLUE PRINT

▨ RED PRINT

□ RED-AND-BLUE PRINT ON OFF-WHITE

This traditional block design is simple to make. Adding borders to a 12"-square block is an easy way to create a cushion cover.

 Cushion Size: 16" x 16"
Finished Block Size: 12" x 12"

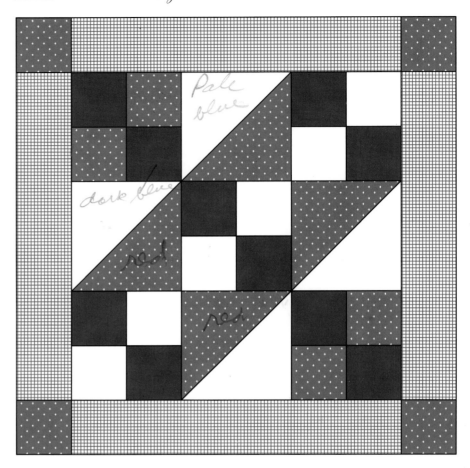

MATERIALS

44"-wide fabric

¼ yd. red print

⅛ yd. blue print

¼ yd. red-and-blue print on off-white

¼ yd. blue-and-off-white check

18" x 18" square of batting

18" x 18" square of lightweight muslin for the lining

18" x 18" fabric square for the cushion back

Fiberfill to fill the cushion or a 16" square pillow form

2 yds. off-white cording or piping

TEMPLATE CUTTING

Use the templates on page 41. All templates and strip measurements include ¼"-wide seam allowances. Cut strips across the fabric width (crosswise grain) unless otherwise noted.

From the red print, cut:

8 squares (Template A)

4 triangles (Template B)

From the blue print, cut:

10 squares (Template A)

From the red-and-blue print on off-white, cut:

6 squares (Template A)

4 triangles (Template B)

From the blue-and-off-white check, cut:

4 strips, each 2½" x 12½", for block borders

ROTARY CUTTING

From the red print, cut:

1 strip, 2½" x 22"; crosscut into 8 squares (A),
    each 2½" x 2½"

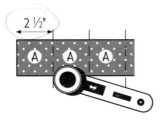

2 squares, each 4⅞" x 4⅞"; cut each square once
    diagonally to yield a total of 4 triangles (B)

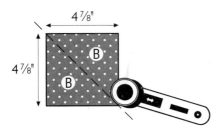

From the blue print, cut:

1 strip, 2½" x 27"; crosscut into 10 squares (A),
    each 2½" x 2½"

From the red-and-blue print on off-white, cut:

1 strip, 2½" x 17"; crosscut into 6 squares (A),
    each 2½" x 2½"

2 squares, each 4⅞" x 4⅞"; cut each square once
    diagonally to yield a total of 4 triangles (B)

From the blue-and-off-white check, cut:

4 strips, each 2½" x 12½", for block borders

PIECING

(by hand or machine)

    See "Sewing Technique" on pages 16–18 for hand
piecing directions.

NOTE

*When piecing by machine, carefully pin the
pieces together for each step and use chain piecing
as shown on page 19 to speed your work.*

1. With right sides together, sew a red-and-blue on off-white square (A) to each of 6 blue squares (A). Press the seams toward the blue squares.

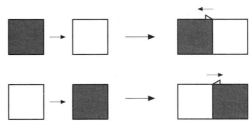

2. To make 3 four-patch units, sew the resulting pieces right sides together in pairs as shown. If hand piecing, press as shown; for machine-pieced units, press the seam allowances in one direction.

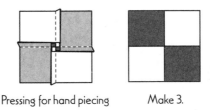

Pressing for hand piecing   Make 3.

3. Repeat steps 1 and 2, using red and blue squares (A) to make 2 four-patch units.

Make 2.

4. To make half-square triangle units, sew each red triangle (B) to a red-and-blue on off-white triangle (B) with right sides together and long edges matching. Make 4 half-square triangle units.

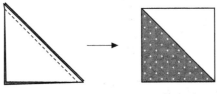

Make 4.

5. Arrange the four-patch units and the half-square triangle units in 3 vertical rows. Sew the blocks together in each row, pressing the seams as indicated by the arrows.

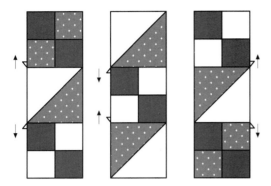

6. Join the rows to complete the block. Add a blue-and-off-white checked strip to opposite sides of the completed block. Press the seams toward the strips.

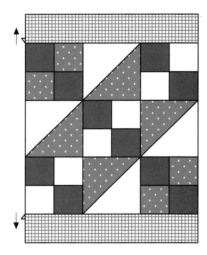

7. Sew a red square (A) to each end of each remaining blue-and-off-white checked strip. Press seams toward the strips. Sew to the remaining sides of the block.

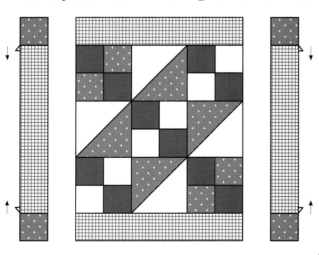

FINISHING

1. Lightly press the completed piece of patchwork.
2. Mark the quilting design, referring to the cushion-top quilting illustration below.

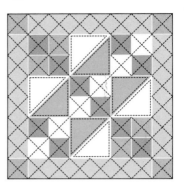

3. Center and layer the cushion top on the batting and the muslin lining; baste.
4. Quilt on the marked lines.
5. Beginning at the center of one side of the quilted cushion top, pin the off-white cording to the top with the seam lines matching. Clip the piping seam allowance to fit it around the corners.

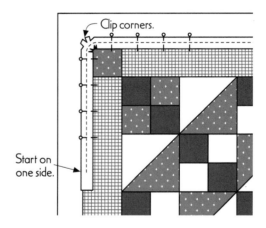

6. When you reach the point where you started, undo the stitches in the cording fabric so you can turn under the end and trim away the excess cord.

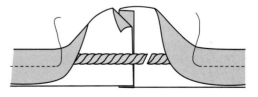

Turn beginning of strip under ¼".
Overlap end. Cut excess cording.

7. Machine stitch, beginning a few inches from the end. Use a zipper foot so you can stitch close to the cording, just inside the piping stitches.

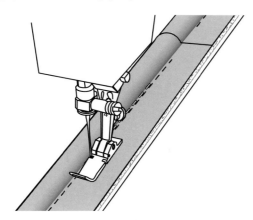

8. Trim batting and muslin even with the edge of the cushion top.

9. Center the completed cushion cover on the square of backing fabric, right sides together; baste. With the lined side of the cushion top facing you, stitch on the first line of stitching, leaving an opening on one edge as shown. Trim the backing even with the edges of the cushion top. Turn the cushion cover right side out.

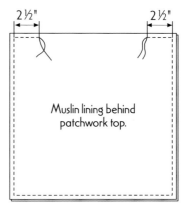

Muslin lining behind patchwork top.

10. Insert the pillow form or stuff with fiberfill and slipstitch the opening edges closed.

Backing

Cording

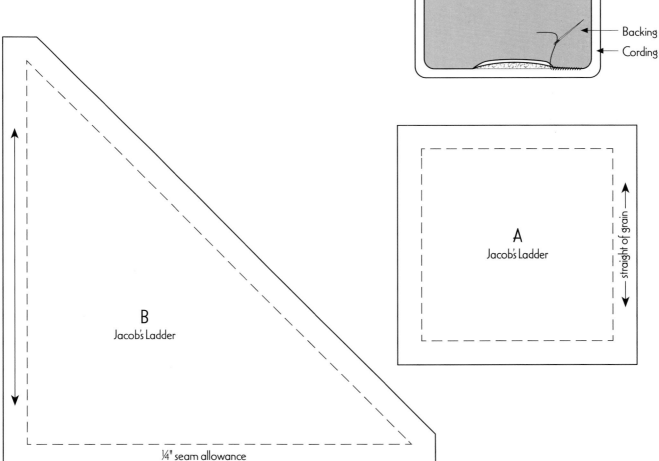

B
Jacob's Ladder

¼" seam allowance

A
Jacob's Ladder

straight of grain

ROMAN STRIPES

Roman Stripes
by Marie-Christine
Flocard,
les Loges en Josas,
France, 1993.
30½" x 40½".
Machine pieced and
hand quilted.

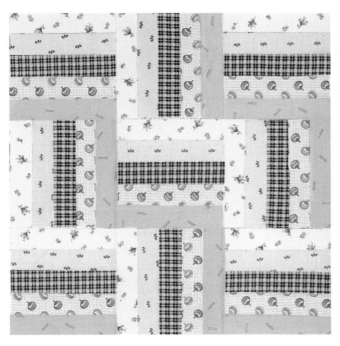

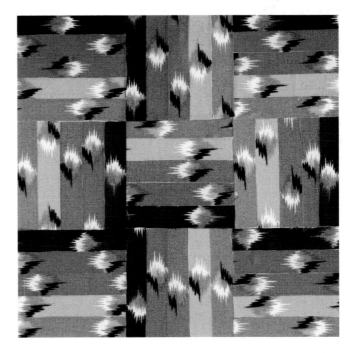

ROMAN STRIPES

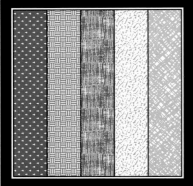

Roman Stripe Block

- **BLUE**
- **PINK**
- **MEDIUM GREEN**
- **YELLOW**
- **LIGHT GREEN**

Select solid fabrics in your favorite color combination to make your own version of this simple-to-sew quilt.

Quilt Size: 30½" x 40½"
Finished Block Size: 5" x 5"

MATERIALS
44"-wide fabric

½ yd. each of light green, medium green, yellow, pink, and blue prints for the blocks and binding

1 yd. for the backing

34" x 44" piece of batting

TEMPLATE CUTTING

Use the template on page 45. All template and strip measurements include ¼"-wide seam allowances.

From the yellow print, cut:
2 strips, each 1¼" x 42", for the binding. Set aside.

From the medium green print, cut:
2 strips, each 1¼" x 42", for the binding. Set aside.

From each of the five prints, cut:
48 rectangles (Template A), totaling 240 rectangles for the blocks

ROTARY CUTTING

Cut strips across the fabric width (crosswise grain). Measurements include ¼"-wide seam allowances.

From the yellow print, cut:

2 strips, each 1¼" x 42", for the binding. Set aside.

From the meduim green print, cut:

2 strips, each 1¼" x 42", for the binding. Set aside.

From each of the five prints, cut:

7 strips, each 1½" x 42", for the blocks

TRADITIONAL PIECING

(by hand or machine)

1. To make each block, join 5 rectangles (A) in the order shown. Make 48 blocks.
2. Press all seams toward the blue strip in each block.

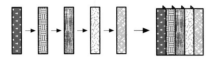

3. To complete your quilt, see "Quilt Top Assembly and Finishing" above right.

MACHINE SPEED PIECING

1. Arrange the strips into 7 identical sets of 5 strips each. Press all seams toward the blue strip in each strip-pieced unit.
2. Cut 5½" squares from each strip-pieced unit for a total of 48 blocks*.

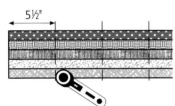

Before cutting squares from the strip-pieced units, measure the width of the units and either adjust the sewing so they do measure 5½" or use the actual measurement instead of 5½" to cut the squares. For example, if the units measure only 5¼", cut squares 5¼" x 5¼".

QUILT TOP ASSEMBLY AND FINISHING

1. Arrange the blocks in 8 rows of 6 blocks each. (Refer to the quilt plan on page 44 and the photo on page 42 for placement.) Check the color placement of each block before proceeding.

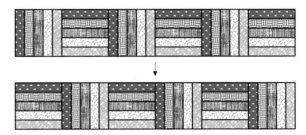

2. Sew the blocks together in horizontal rows and press the seams open between the blocks. Sew the rows together and press seams open.
3. Lightly press the completed quilt top.
4. Mark quilting lines across both diagonals of each block as shown.

5. Layer the quilt top with batting and backing; baste. See pages 24–25.
6. Quilt on the marked lines.
7. Bind one long edge with a green-print binding strip and the other with a yellow-print strip, following the "Method One" directions on pages 28–29 for attaching binding. Repeat with the remaining edges, alternating colors around the quilt.

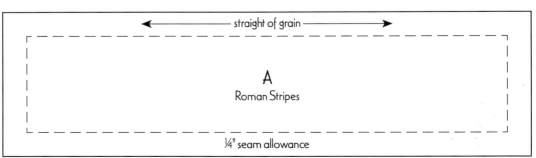

straight of grain

A
Roman Stripes

¼" seam allowance

FOUR PATCHES

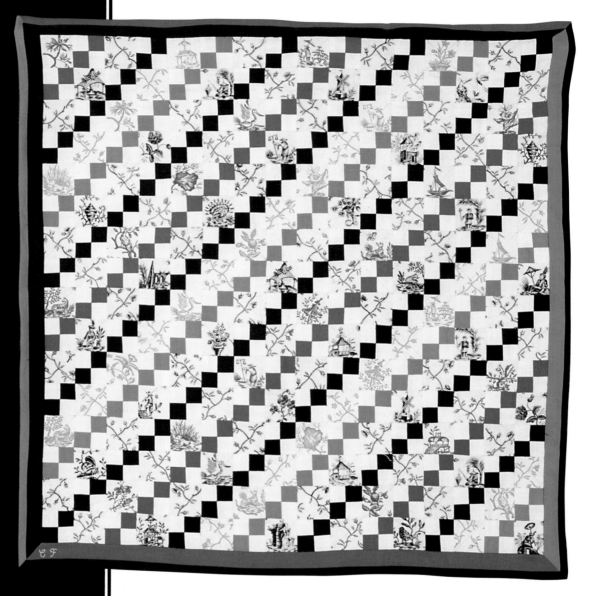

Four Patches
by Marie-Christine Flocard,
les Loges en Josas, France,
1993.
27½" x 27½".
Machine pieced and
hand quilted.

FOUR PATCHES

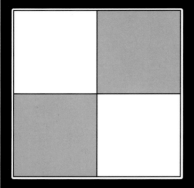

Four Patch Block

 CORAL PRINT

 CORAL SOLID

 DARK GREEN PRINT

 DARK GREEN SOLID

 GOLD PRINT

 GOLD SOLID

 NAVY BLUE PRINT

 NAVY BLUE SOLID

 OFF-WHITE

To create diagonal bands of color, Marie-Christine's simple Four Patch quilt requires careful attention to color placement.

 Quilt Size: 27½" x 27½"
Finished Block Size: 1½" x 1½"

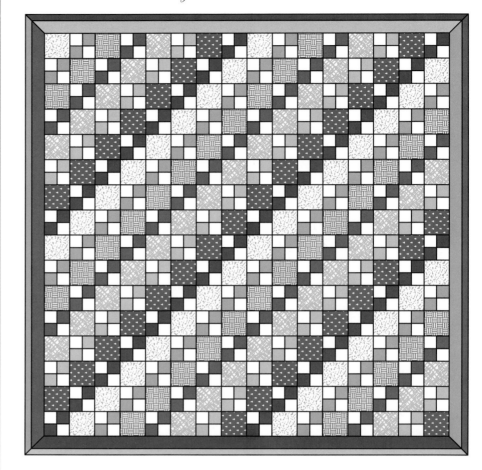

MATERIALS
44"-wide fabric

¼ yd. each of solid coral, navy blue, dark green, and gold for the Four Patch blocks

½ yd. off-white solid for the Four Patch blocks

¼ yd. each of 4 different prints for the alternate squares; choose fabrics with an off-white background with printed designs in colors that match the solid colors*

⅞ yd. for the backing

31½" x 31½" piece of batting

¼ yd. for binding (optional**)

*Marie-Christine used a toile de Jouy print called Pillement for the squares. This French fabric is only 1 meter wide and so required additional yardage.

**In the quilt shown, Marie-Christine actually turned the edge of the outer border to the back of the quilt as described for turning the backing to the front in "Self-Binding" on page 30.

TEMPLATE CUTTING

Use the templates on page 50. All templates and strip measurements include ¼"-wide seam allowances.

From each of the solid-color fabrics, cut:

2 strips, each 1¼" x 30", for a total of 8 strips. Set aside for the borders.

64 squares (Template A), for a total of 256

From the off-white, cut:

256 squares (Template A)

From each of the prints, cut:

32 squares (Template B), for a total of 128

ROTARY CUTTING

Cut strips across the fabric width (crosswise grain). Measurements include ¼"-wide seam allowances.

From each of the solid-color fabrics, cut:

4 strips, each 1¼" x 42". Set 2 of each aside for the borders.

From the off-white fabric, cut:

8 strips, each 1¼" x 42"

From each of the prints, cut:

2 strips, each 2" x 42". Crosscut strips into squares, each 2" x 2". You need 32 squares of each print for a total of 128. A portion of one strip of each print will be left over. Set aside for other quilt projects.

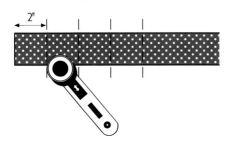

TRADITIONAL PIECING

(by hand or machine)

1. Sew a solid-color square (A) to an off-white square (A). Press the seam toward the solid-color square. Repeat with all remaining squares.

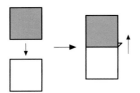

2. Sew 2 sets of matching squares together to make a Four Patch block. Repeat with the remaining pieces to make a total of 128 blocks.

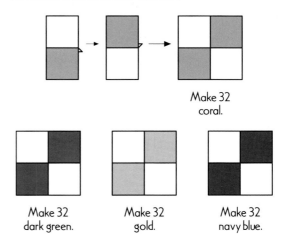

Make 32 coral.

Make 32 dark green.

Make 32 gold.

Make 32 navy blue.

3. To complete your quilt, see "Quilt Top Assembly and Finishing" on page 50.

MACHINE SPEED PIECING

1. Sew each 1¼"-wide coral strip to a 1¼"-wide off-white strip. Press the seam toward the coral fabric in each strip-pieced unit. Crosscut the units into 1¼"-wide segments. You need a total of 64 segments.

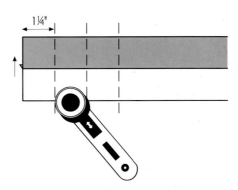

2. Sew two segments together to create a Four Patch block as shown in step 2 of "Traditional Piecing" above. Continue with the remaining segments to make a total of 32 blocks. Chain piece if desired. See page 19. Each block should measure 2" x 2".

3. Repeat steps 1 and 2, using the remaining off-white strips and 2 strips each of the navy blue, dark green, and gold strips. You need 32 blocks of each color for a total of 128 blocks.

4. To complete your quilt, see "Quilt Top Assembly and Finishing" on page 50.

QUILT TOP ASSEMBLY AND FINISHING

1. Arrange the blocks and print squares (B) in 16 rows. (Refer to the quilt plan on page 48 and the photo on page 46 for placement.) Alternate 8 Four Patch blocks with 8 print squares in each row. Check the color placement of each block and square before proceeding.

2. Sew the blocks together in horizontal rows. Press the seams in opposite directions from row to row. Sew the rows of blocks together.

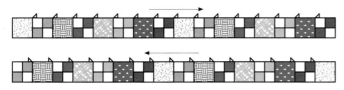

Press seams in direction of arrows.

3. Sew a coral strip to a dark green strip. Repeat with the gold and the navy blue strips. Press the seam toward the darker fabric in each strip-pieced unit.

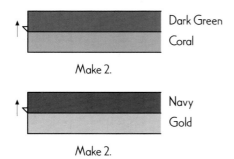

4. Referring to the quilt plan and the quilt photo for color placement, sew the completed border units to the quilt top as described on pages 21–22 for "Borders with Mitered Corners."

5. Lightly press the completed quilt top.

6. Mark quilting lines across the diagonals of each print square.

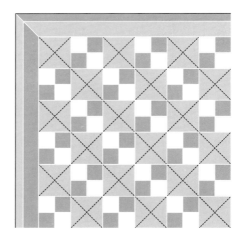

7. Layer the quilt top with batting and backing; baste. (See pages 24–25.)

8. Quilt on the marked lines.

9. Finish the quilt with the binding method of your choice. See "Adding Binding" on pages 28–30.

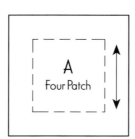

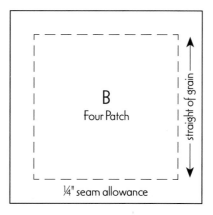

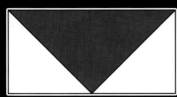

FLYING GEESE

Flying Geese Block

Will made the quilt in the photo on page 52 from a variety of scraps totaling approximately two yards. The materials list at right calls for six different print fabrics.

Quilt Size: 59½" x 90¼"
Finished Block Size: 1¾" x 3½"

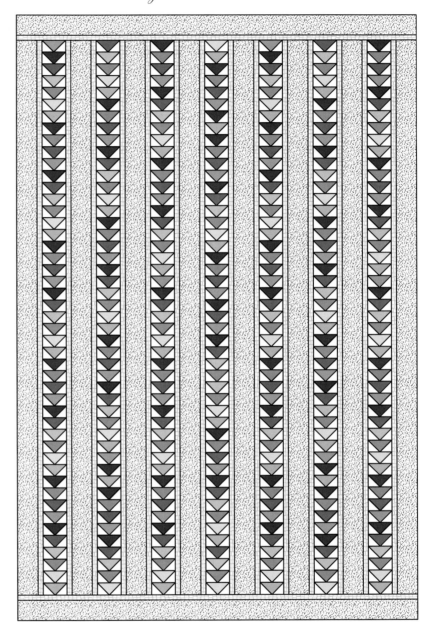

MATERIALS
44"-wide fabric

⅓ yd. each of 6 different prints for
  Flying Geese blocks
1⅝ yds. off-white solid if template
  cutting Flying Geese blocks
OR
2¾ yds. off-white solid if rotary
  cutting Flying Geese blocks*
2½ yds. blue solid for alternating
  strips

1½ yds. yellow solid for the
  sashing
⅓ yd. yellow print for the binding
5½ yds. for backing
64" x 94" piece of batting

Rotary cutting requires additional yardage. There will be some waste with the piecing method shown, but the time saved is worth it!

FLYING GEESE

Flying Geese
by
Willemke Vidinic,
Paris, France,
1987.
59½" x 90¼".
Machine pieced and
hand quilted.

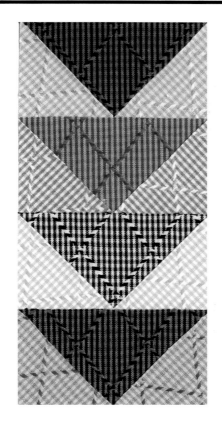

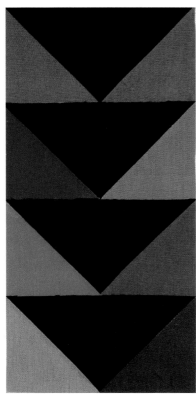

TEMPLATE CUTTING

Use the templates on page 56. All templates and strip measurements include ¼"-wide seam allowances. Cut all strips across the fabric width (crosswise grain).

From each of the 6 prints, cut:

55 triangles (Template A), tracing the templates in the arrangement shown to save fabric. You need a total of 329 triangles.

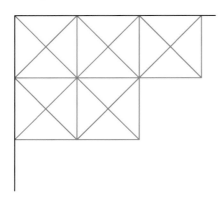

From the off-white solid, cut:

658 triangles (Template B), tracing the templates in the arrangement shown to save fabric

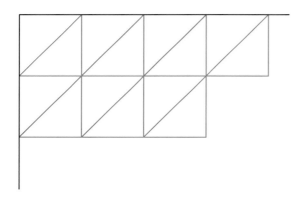

From the blue solid, cut:

8 strips, each 3½" x 80", for the alternate strips and the borders. Cut strips from the length of the fabric.

2 strips, each 3½" x 62", for the top and bottom borders. Cut strips from the length of the fabric.

From the yellow solid, cut:

32 strips, each 1¼" x 42", for the sashing

From the yellow print, cut:

8 strips, each 1¼" x 42", for the binding

ROTARY CUTTING

Cut all strips across the fabric width (crosswise grain), unless otherwise noted. All strip measurements include ¼"-wide seam allowances.

From the off-white, cut:

35 strips, each 2¼" x 42"; crosscut into a total of 658 squares, each 2¼" x 2¼"

From each of the 6 prints, cut:

5 strips, each 2¼" x 42"; crosscut each set of strips into a total of 55 rectangles, each 2¼" x 4". Cut a total of 330 rectangles. You need only 329 rectangles to complete the quilt, so set one aside for another quilt project.

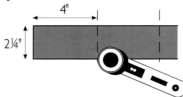

From the blue solid, cut:

8 strips, each 3½" x 80", for the alternate strips and borders. Cut strips from the length of the fabric.

2 strips, each 3½" x 62", for the top and bottom borders. Cut strips from the length of the fabric.

From the yellow solid, cut:

32 strips, each 1¼" x 42", for the sashing

From the yellow print, cut:

8 strips, each 1¼" x 42", for the binding

TRADITIONAL PIECING

1. Sew 2 off-white triangles (B) to each print triangle (A). Make 329 Flying Geese blocks.

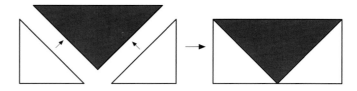

2. Press the seams toward the outer triangle, unless they show through the fabric too much. If so, press them toward the center triangle.

3. Arrange the completed Flying Geese blocks into 7 vertical rows of 47 blocks each. Sew the blocks together in rows and press each seam toward the long edge of the next block. Assemble the quilt, following the directions for "Quilt Top Assembly" below right.

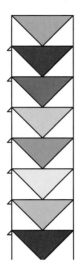

MACHINE SPEED PIECING

1. Using a sharp pencil and a ruler, draw a diagonal line on the wrong side of each off-white square.

2. With right sides together, sew an off-white square to the left corner of a print rectangle, stitching on the diagonal line.

3. Sew an off-white square to the left corner of each remaining print rectangle in the same manner, chain piecing to save time. (See page 19.)

4. Trim away the lower corner of each square and rectangle ¼" from the stitching line. Press remaining triangle toward the lower left corner of the rectangle.

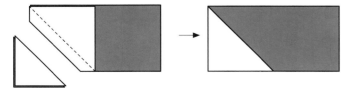

5. Repeat steps 3 and 4, sewing a square to the right end of each remaining rectangle. Pay careful attention to the position of the diagonal line. You need a total of 329 Flying Geese blocks.

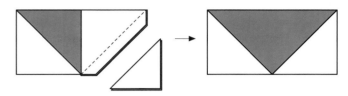

6. Arrange the blocks and sew into 7 vertical rows of 47 blocks each as described in step 3 for "Traditional Piecing" above left.

QUILT TOP ASSEMBLY

1. Measure the completed strips. They should all be the same length. If there are wide variations in length, adjust the lengths by taking slightly deeper or narrower seams between a few blocks.

2. Cut the eight 3½" x 80" long blue strips to match the length of the Flying Geese strips.

3. For sashing, sew the yellow-solid strips together, end to end, in sets of 2. Press the seams open. You need 16 long strips. Set 2 strips aside. Cut the remaining 14 strips to match the length of the blue strips.

4. Sew a yellow sashing strip to each edge of each Flying Geese strip. Press the seams toward the yellow strips.

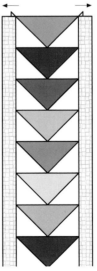

5. Referring to the quilt plan and the color photo, arrange the Flying Geese strips with the blue strips, beginning and ending with a blue strip. Join the strips and press the seams toward the blue strips.

6. Measure the quilt top through the center horizontally. Cut the 2 remaining yellow-solid strips to match this measurement. Sew one strip each to the top and bottom edges of the quilt top. Press the seams toward the yellow strips.

7. Repeat step 6 with the 3½" x 62" blue strips, cutting them to fit the top and bottom edges of the quilt top. Sew to the top and bottom edges of the quilt top. Press the seams toward the blue strips.

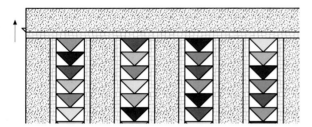

FINISHING

1. Lightly press the completed quilt top.

2. Mark the quilt top with the desired design. In the quilt pictured, the quilting was done approximately ⅛" from the seam line inside each off-white triangle and an interlocking diamond design was quilted in the long blue strips. Quilting was done ¼" from the seam line inside the yellow sashing strips.

3. Cut the backing fabric into two pieces of equal length. Cut one length in half lengthwise and sew the halves to the long edges of the remaining piece. Press the seams open. Trim to 64" x 94".

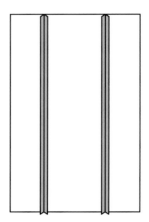

4. Layer the quilt top with batting and backing; baste. (See pages 24–25.)

5. Quilt on the marked lines.

6. Sew the yellow-print binding strips together in pairs, end to end, to make 4 strips. Bind the edges of the quilt, following the "Method One" directions on pages 28–29 for attaching binding.

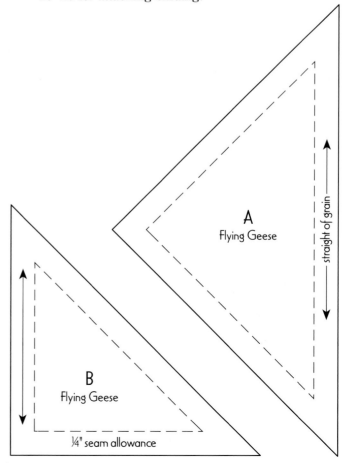

A
Flying Geese

straight of grain

B
Flying Geese

¼" seam allowance

LOG CABIN

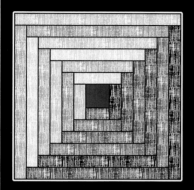

Log Cabin Block

Willemke Vidinic used about forty different over-dyed-jeans fabrics to make the quilt shown in the photo on page 58. To obtain similar results, use light and dark solid-colored scraps or buy small amounts of assorted fabrics. You need twelve different light solids in yellow, gray, light brown, beige, and green and twelve different dark solids in black, green, blue, brown, rust, and gray. Substitute prints if you prefer.

 Quilt Size: 57½" x 57½"
Finished Block Size: 7½" x 7½"

MATERIALS
44"-wide fabric

⅓ yd. each of 12 different light fabrics and 12 different dark fabrics (24 fabrics total)

¼ yd. red solid for the chimneys (squares in the center)

2½ yds. lightweight muslin for the block foundations*

3½ yds. for the backing**

*The "logs" in this quilt are stitched to squares of foundation fabric. Batting is normally not used due to the thickness of the seams under the narrow logs in the blocks; the foundation squares act as the "filler."

**The backing is brought to the front of the quilt for self binding (See page 30). Take care to use a color that coordinates well with the others you have chosen.

LOG CABIN

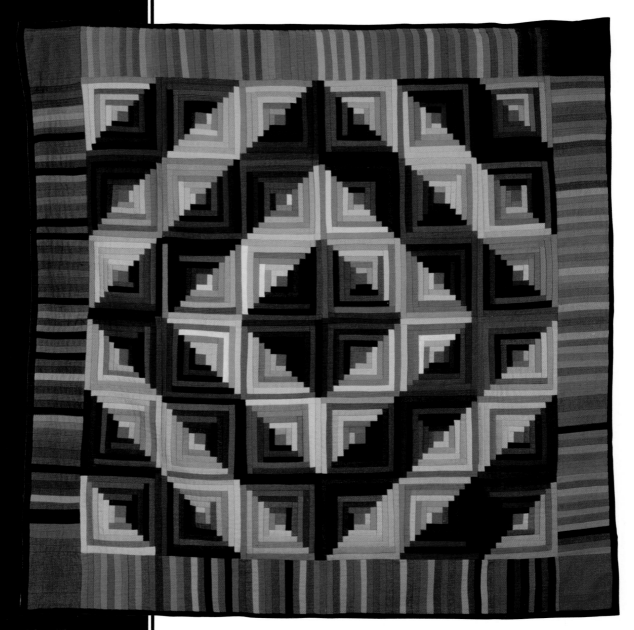

*Log Cabin
by Willemke Vidinic,
Paris, France, 1992.
57 ½" x 57 ½".
Machine pieced and
hand quilted.*

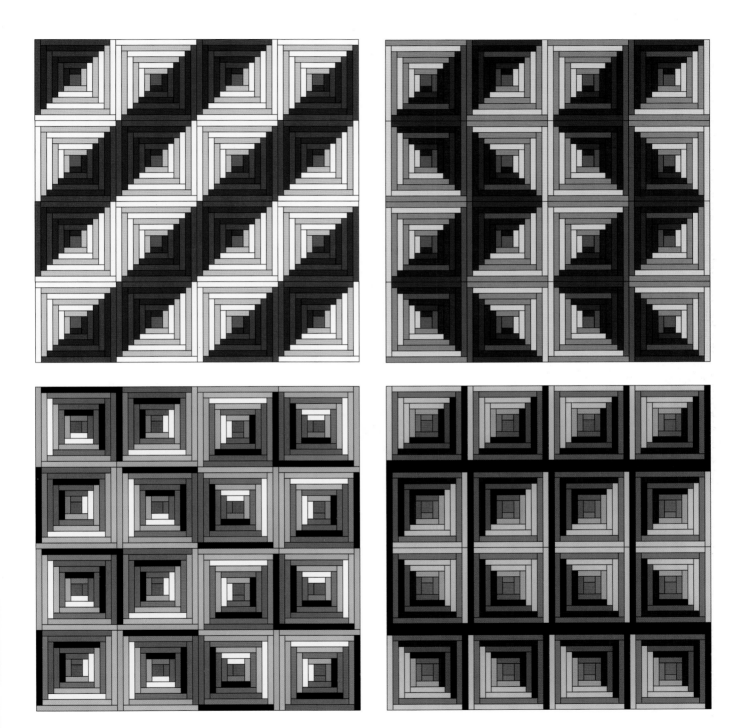

ROTARY CUTTING*

Cut all strips across the width of the fabric (crosswise grain). All strip measurements include ¼"-wide seam allowances.

Templates are not necessary for this quilt since the pattern requires strips of the same width cut from a variety of fabrics.

From each of the 12 light fabrics, cut:

6 to 8 strips, each 1" x 42", for the blocks and borders; cut additional strips as needed

From each of 4 of the dark fabrics, *first* cut:

1 square, 6½" x 6½", for a total of 4 squares for the corners

From each of the 12 dark fabrics, cut:

6 to 8 strips, each 1" x 42", for the blocks and borders; cut additional strips as needed.

From the red solid, cut:

2 strips, each 2" x 42"; crosscut into 2" squares. You need 36 squares, one for the center of each block.

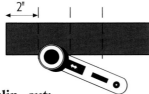

From the muslin, cut:

9 strips, each 8½" x 42"; crosscut into 8½" squares. You need 36 squares for the block foundations.

PIECING

(by hand or machine)

Make 36 Log Cabin blocks.

1. Draw diagonal lines from corner to corner on a muslin square.

Muslin foundation

2. Center a red square on top of the muslin square, right side up, making sure that each of the 4 corners of the red square touches a diagonal line. Pin.

3. With right sides together and raw edges matching, pin a strip of light fabric to one edge of the red square. Stitch ¼" from the raw edges. Trim the strip even with the red square. Remove the pins.

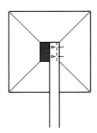

4. Turn the strip onto the muslin square and press. Pin in place.

5. Rotate the block counterclockwise and sew a light strip to the block in the same manner. Use the same light strip or another light strip of a similar color. Trim, press, and pin as you did for the first strip.

6. Continuing to rotate the block counterclockwise, sew 2 dark strips to the block in the same manner as you did the 2 light strips.

7. Continue rotating the block and adding sets of light and dark strips until you have added a total of 6 light strips and 6 dark strips as shown in the block illustration on page 57. Press the completed blocks.

8. Measure your completed blocks but do not include excess muslin foundation. They should all measure 8" square. Then, using a rotary cutter and ruler, trim the foundation square even with the outer edges of the block so that it measures 8" square. If some

blocks are much smaller than others, trim them so all are the same size. (Remember to trim a little from each side, rather than trimming the entire amount from only one side of the block.)

QUILT TOP ASSEMBLY

1. Arrange the blocks in 6 rows of 6 blocks each. (Refer to the quilt plan on page 57 and the photo on page 58 for placement.) Sew the blocks together in rows, pressing the seams in opposite directions from row to row.

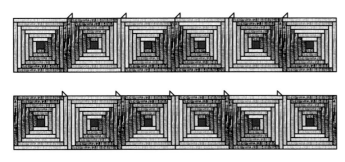

2. Sew the rows together.

PIECED BORDERS

1. Sew any remaining 1"-wide strips together in a random arrangement of colors. Press all seams in one direction. From the strip-pieced unit (or units), cut strips 6½" wide.

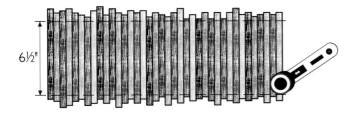

2. For each side of the quilt, sew enough 6½"-wide strips together to make a 6½" x 45½" strip. Each of the 4 border strips required will have a total of 90 strips in it. If necessary, cut additional 1"-wide strips from light and dark fabrics left from making the blocks.

3. Sew a pieced border to opposite sides of the quilt top and press the seam toward the quilt top. Sew a dark square to each short end of the 2 remaining pieced borders and press the seam toward the border strip. Sew borders to the remaining sides of the quilt top.

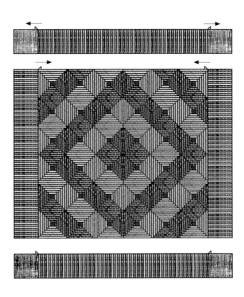

FINISHING

1. Lightly press the completed quilt top.

2. Cut the backing fabric into two pieces of equal length. From one of the pieces, cut 2 strips, each 11" wide. Sew to the long edges of the other piece of backing. Press seams open.

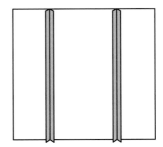

3. Center the quilt top on the backing, wrong sides together. Baste.

4. Quilt in-the-ditch around the chimney and each Log Cabin block.

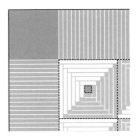

5. Trim the backing so that it extends ½" beyond the edge of the quilt top.

6. Bind the edges of the quilt with the backing as shown in "Self Binding" on page 30.

NINEPATCHES

Ninepatches
by Willemke Vidinic,
Paris, France, 1991.
80" x 80".
Machine pieced
and hand quilted.

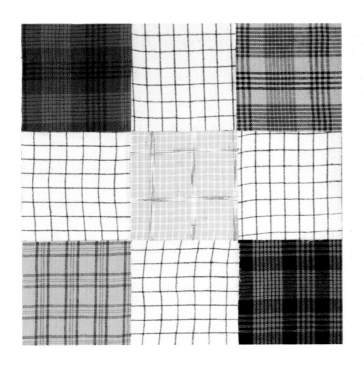

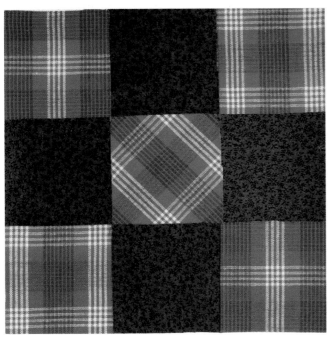

NINEPATCHES

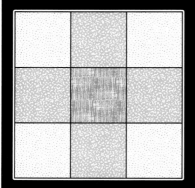

Ninepatch Block

This quilt was made with a variety of printed-fabric scraps (checks, stripes, and dots) in blue, beige, brown, red, gray, and black. The materials list includes a variety of fabrics so that you can make a scrappy quilt even if you don't have scraps.

Quilt Size: 80" x 80"
Finished Block Size: 7½" x 7½"

MATERIALS
44"-wide fabric
⅜ yd. each of 12 different prints for the Ninepatch blocks
⅓ yd. each of 6 different prints (predominately shades of blue) for the triangles
⅓ yd. red-and-white plaid for the inner border
⅞ yd. blue striped fabric for the outer border
4¾ yds. for the backing
⅓ yd. red print for the binding
85" x 85" piece of batting

TEMPLATE CUTTING
Use the templates on page 67. All templates and strip measurements include ¼"-wide seam allowances. Cut all strips across the fabric width (crosswise grain).

From each of 3 of the prints for the Ninepatch blocks, cut:

36 squares (Template A), for a total of 108 squares

From each of the remaining 9 prints for the blocks, cut:

34 squares (Template A), for a total of 306 squares

From each of the 6 prints for the triangles, cut:

16 triangles (Template B), for a total of 96 triangles

From each of 4 of the triangle fabrics, cut:
2 triangles (Template C), for a total of 8 triangles
From the remaining 2 triangle fabrics, cut:
4 triangles each (Template C), for a total of 8 triangles
From the red-and-white plaid, cut:
8 strips, each 1" x 42", for the inner border
From the blue striped fabric, cut:
8 strips, each 3" x 42", for the outer border
From the red print, cut:
8 strips, each 1¼" x 42", for the binding

ROTARY CUTTING

All measurements include ¼"-wide seam allowances. Cut all strips across the fabric width (crosswise grain).
From the 12 prints for the Ninepatch blocks, cut:
a total of 414 squares, each 3" x 3"*
From the 6 prints for the triangles, cut:
a total of 24 squares, each 17" x
17"*; cut twice diagonally
to yield 96 large triangles
with the straight of grain
along the longest side
8 squares, each 6¼" x 6¼"*;
cut once diagonally to
yield 16 small triangles
with the straight of grain
along the two short sides

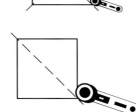

If you wish, first cut strips of the appropriate width, then crosscut into the required squares.
From the red-and-white plaid, cut:
8 strips, each 1" x 42", for the inner border
From the blue striped fabric, cut:
8 strips, each 3" x 42", for the outer border
From the red-and-white print, cut:
8 strips, each 1¼" x 42", for the binding

N O T E
*If you prefer to work with fewer colors
for a less scrappy quilt, quick-piece Ninepatch
blocks on the machine. To do this, cut and assemble
strip-pieced units of the desired colors, then cut them
into segments to join into blocks. If you wish to
quick-piece in this fashion, cut 3"-wide strips from
the desired fabrics and follow the directions under
"Quick-Piecing Ninepatch Blocks" on page 66.
The number of strips required depends
on the number of fabrics you use.*

PIECING
(by hand or machine)

1. Arrange the squares in 46 blocks of 9 squares each in the desired color combinations. (Refer to the quilt plan on page 64 and the quilt photo on page 62.)
2. For each block, sew together 3 rows of 3 squares each. Press seams in opposite directions from row to row as indicated by the arrows in the illustration.

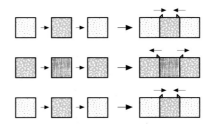

3. Sew the rows together and press the seams in one direction. You need 46 Ninepatch blocks.

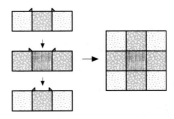

QUILT TOP ASSEMBLY

1. Referring to the quilt plan and the color photo, arrange the completed Ninepatch blocks and the large and small triangles in 7 vertical rows. Odd-numbered rows begin and end with small triangles (C). Even rows begin and end with large triangles (B).
2. Sew the blocks and triangles in each row together in diagonal sections as shown. Press the seams toward the triangles.

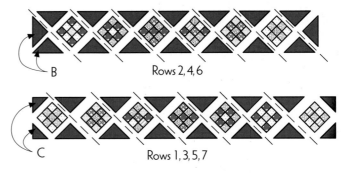

Rows 2, 4, 6

Rows 1, 3, 5, 7

3. Join the completed rows and press the seams in one direction.
4. Sew 2 red-and-white checked border strips together, end to end; press the seam open. Repeat with the

remaining red-and-white checked strips to make 4 inner-border strips. Make 4 outer-border strips in the same manner, using the blue-striped strips.

5. Measure the quilt top for borders with straight-cut corners as shown on page 21. Cut 2 red-and-white plaid strips to this measurement. Sew to opposite sides of the quilt top. Measure, cut, and attach border strips to the remaining sides of the quilt top.

6. Measure, cut, and sew the blue-striped outer borders to the quilt top in the same manner.

FINISHING

1. Lightly press the completed quilt top.
2. Mark the quilt top for quilting. Mark diagonal lines through the square in each Ninepatch block. Mark stitching lines ¼" from the seam lines in each setting triangle.

3. Layer the quilt top with batting and backing; baste. (See pages 24–25.)
4. Quilt on the marked lines.
5. Bind the edges with the straight-cut, red-print binding strips. Use your choice of Methods One or Two on pages 28–30.

QUICK-PIECING NINEPATCH BLOCKS

The directions that follow illustrate strip-pieced units for blocks composed of two colors. The finished size of the blocks in this example is 7½" x 7½". Cut strips 3" wide.

1. Assemble one strip unit; use 2 strips of Color #1 and 1 strip of Color #2. Press the seams toward the darker strips as indicated by the arrows in the illustration.

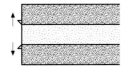

2. Assemble another strip unit, using 2 strips of Color #2 and 1 strip of Color #1. Press the seams toward the darker strip.

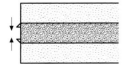

3. Cut 3"-wide segments from the strip-pieced units.

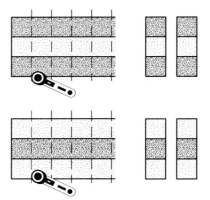

4. Arrange 3 segments to create a Ninepatch block. Sew the segments together.

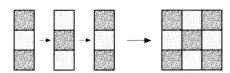

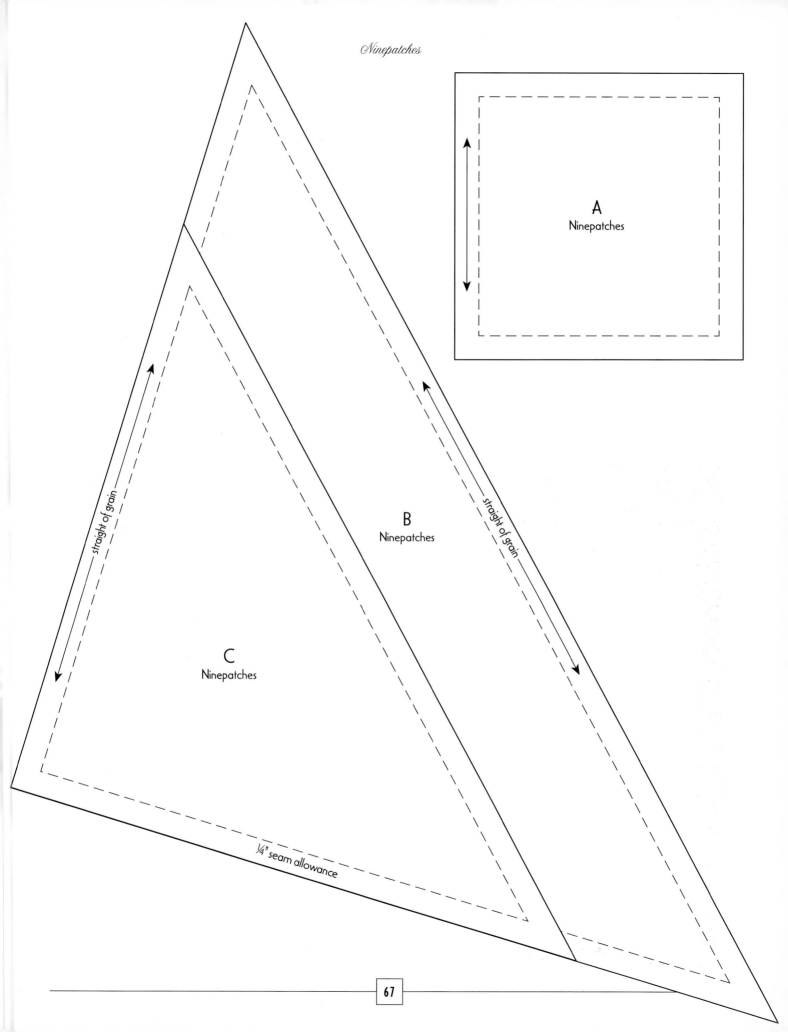

A
Ninepatches

B
Ninepatches

C
Ninepatches

straight of grain

straight of grain

¼" seam allowance

COUNTRY MEDALLION

Country Medallion by Cosabeth Parriaud, Paris, France, 1993. 52½" x 52½". Machine pieced and hand quilted.

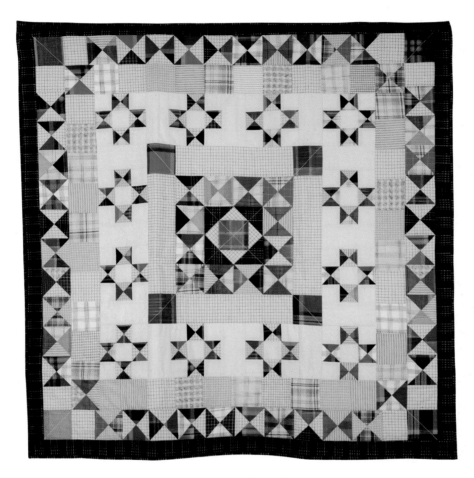

Country Medallion
(variation)
by Soizik Labbens, Nantes, France, 1993.
52½" x 52½".

Quilt Size: 52½" x 52½"
Finished Block Sizes: I: 8" x 8". II: 4" x 4". III: 6" x 6"

COUNTRY MEDALLION

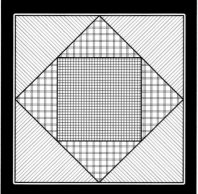

Block I—3 fabrics

Block II—2 fabrics

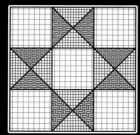

Block III—3 fabrics

Cosabeth used three classic blocks—Square-in-a-Square, Hourglass, and Ohio Star—to create this colorful, scrappy quilt.

MATERIALS
44"-wide fabric
⅝ yd. green-and-off-white check
⅜ yd. each of 11 assorted striped and checked fabrics in red, green, beige, and off-white
¼ yd. dark green solid for the binding
3 yds. for the backing
56" x 56" piece of batting

TEMPLATE CUTTING
Use the templates on page 74. All templates and strip measurements include ¼"-wide seam allowances. Cut all strips across the fabric width (crosswise grain).

From the green-and-off-white check, cut:
4 strips, each 4½" x 16½", for the center-medallion border
From the assorted fabrics, including the remainder of the green-and-off-white check, cut a total of:
69 squares (Template A)
148 triangles (Template B)
4 triangles (Template C), each cut from the same fabric
12 rectangles (Template D)
60 squares (Template E)
192 triangles (Template F)
From the green solid, cut:
6 strips, each 1¼" x 42", for the binding

NOTE

To lighten the patchwork, cut a higher proportion of pieces from the green-and-off-white check than from the other eleven fabrics.

ROTARY CUTTING

From the green-and-off-white check, cut:
4 strips, each 4½" x 16½", for the center-medallion border

From the assorted fabrics, including the remainder of the green-and-off-white check, cut a total of:
69 squares (A), each 4½" x 4½"
37 squares, each 5¼" x 5¼"; cut each square twice diagonally for a total of 148 triangles (B)

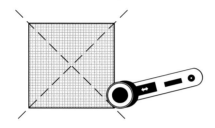

2 squares of the same fabric, each 4⅞" x 4⅞"; cut once diagonally for 4 matching triangles (C)

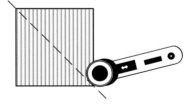

12 rectangles (D), each 4½" x 6½"
60 squares (E), each 2½" x 2½"
96 squares, each 2⅜" x 2⅜". Cut each square once diagonally for a total of 192 triangles (F)

From the green solid, cut:
6 strips, each 1¼" x 42", for the binding

PIECING
(by hand or machine)

Piece each of the three different blocks required for this quilt, following the directions below. If you machine piece, we recommend using chain piecing, shown on page 19, to speed your work.

Block I

Use 3 different fabrics for this block, which will be the center medallion.

1. Choose 4 triangles (B) of the same color. Sew 2 triangles to opposite sides of a checked square (A), then sew two triangles to the remaining sides. Press the seams toward the triangles.

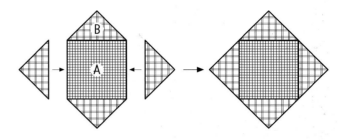

2. Add 4 triangles (C), all the same color, in the same manner.

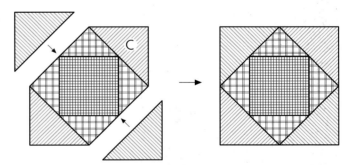

Block II

Use two different fabrics in each of these blocks. Make 36 Block II.

1. For each block arrange 4 triangles (B), 2 each of 2 different fabrics, in an hourglass shape.

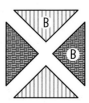

2. Sew the triangles together in pairs and press the seam toward the darker fabric in each pair.

3. Join the triangle pairs to complete the block. Pin carefully at the seam intersection to ensure a perfect match. Press.

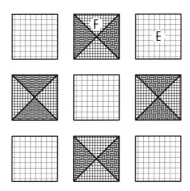

Block III

Use 3 different fabrics in each of these blocks. Make 12 Block III.

1. Arrange each block, using 5 squares (E) of the same fabric and 8 triangles (F) each of two different fabrics.

2. Sew the triangles together to make 4 units for each block as shown in steps 2 and 3 for Block II.
3. Sew the squares and blocks together in rows, pressing the seams as shown by the arrows. Sew the rows together to complete each block.

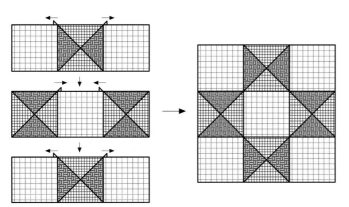

CENTRAL MEDALLION ASSEMBLY

1. Arrange 12 Block II of your choice around Block I. Sew 2 Block II together; sew this unit to the top edge of Block I. Repeat for the bottom edge of Block I. Join 4 Block II for each remaining side of Block I and sew in place.

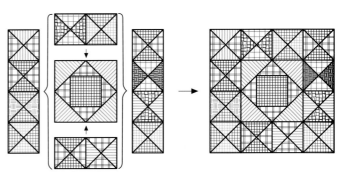

2. Add one green-and-off-white 4½" x 16½" strip each to the top and bottom edges of the center block. Press the seams toward the strips.

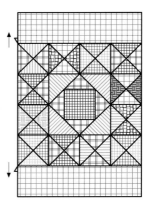

3. Sew a square (A) to opposite ends of each of the remaining green-and-off-white strips. Press the seams toward the strips. Use 4 different colors for the squares. Sew to the sides of the center medallion.

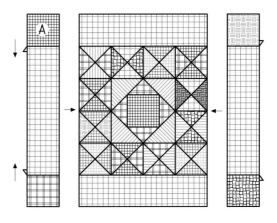

QUILT TOP ASSEMBLY

1. Arrange 12 rectangles (D) and 12 Block III around the central medallion. Sew the pieces together as shown. Add the completed strips to the top and bottom edges and then to the sides of the medallion.

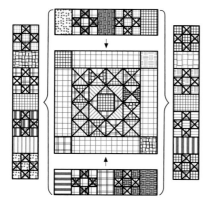

2. For the next round, arrange 40 squares (A) around the quilt top. Sew the pieces together as shown. Add the completed strips to the top and bottom edges and then to the sides of the medallion.

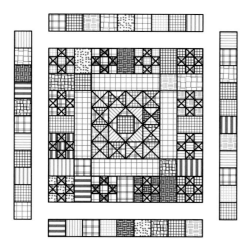

3. For the last round, arrange the remaining 24 squares (A) with the remaining 24 Block II as shown. Sew the pieces together and add the completed strips to the top and bottom edges and then to the sides of the medallion as shown above right.

FINISHING

1. Lightly press the completed quilt top.
2. Mark the blocks for quilting as shown.

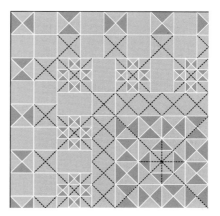

3. Cut the backing fabric into 2 pieces of equal length. Cut 2 strips, each 9" wide, from one of the 2 pieces. Sew these pieces to the long sides of the remaining piece of backing. Press the seams open.

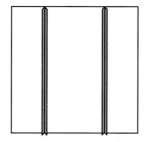

4. Layer the quilt top with batting and backing; baste. See "Layering the Quilt" on pages 24–25.
5. Quilt on the marked lines.
6. Bind the edges with the green strips. Use your choice of binding methods shown on pages 28–30.

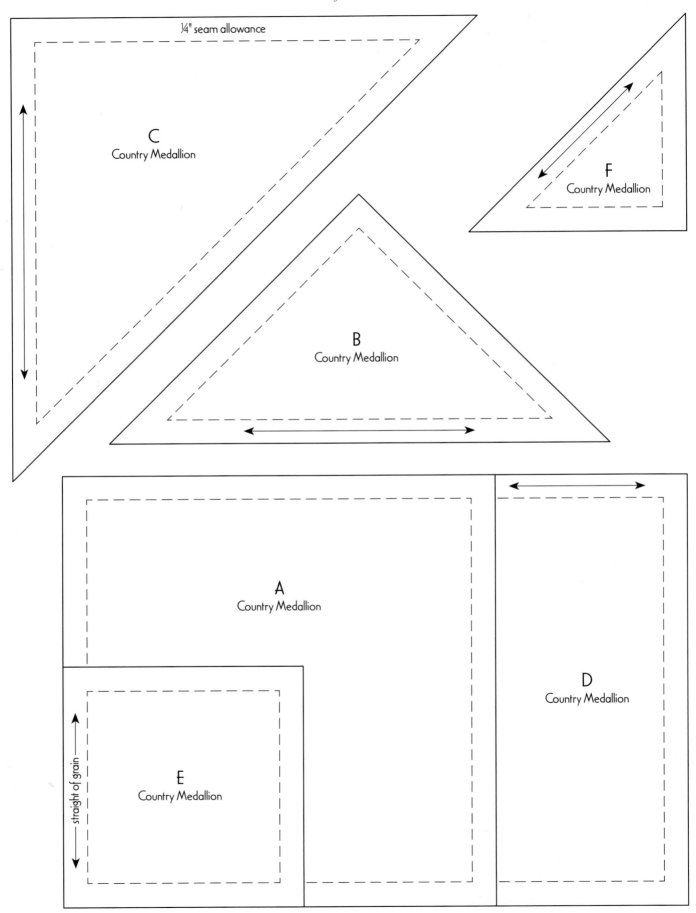

C
Country Medallion

¼" seam allowance

F
Country Medallion

B
Country Medallion

A
Country Medallion

D
Country Medallion

E
Country Medallion

straight of grain

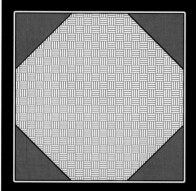

DUTCH TILES

Dutch Tile

ASSORTED PLAIDS, CHECKS AND STRIPES

RUST

LIGHT BLUE

MEDIUM BLUE

DARK BLUE

NAVY BLUE

YELLOW-BROWN

GOLD

This block, an octagon surrounded by four triangles, consists of five squares (one big and four small ones). It is traditionally known as a Snowball block.

 Quilt Size: 48½" x 48½"
Finished Block Size: 6" x 6"

MATERIALS
44"-wide fabric

¼ yd. each of 16 different plaid, checked, and striped fabrics
⅓ yd. rust solid
⅛ yd. light blue solid
⅛ yd. dark blue solid
¼ yd. medium blue solid
¼ yd. navy blue solid
¼ yd. yellow-brown solid
¼ yd. gold solid
2¾ yds. for the backing
52" x 52" piece of batting

TEMPLATE CUTTING

Use the templates on page 80. All templates and strip measurements include ¼"-wide seam allowances. Cut all strips across the fabric width (crosswise grain).

From each of the 16 different plaid, checked, and striped fabrics, cut:

4 squares (Template A). You need a total of 64 squares.

From the solid-color fabrics, cut:

the squares (Template B) indicated below, for a total of 256 squares
80 rust
16 light blue
16 dark blue
48 medium blue
32 navy blue
32 yellow-brown
32 gold

To cut binding strips, see step 8 in "Quilt Top Assembly and Finishing" on page 79.

DUTCH TILES

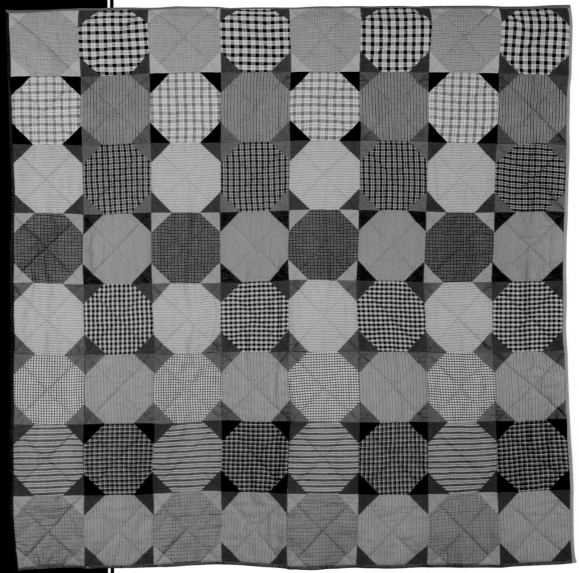

*Dutch Tiles
by Marie-Christine Flocard,
les Loges en Josas, France,
1993.
48½" x 48½".
Machine pieced
and hand quilted.*

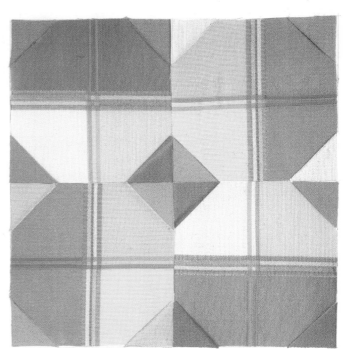

ROTARY CUTTING

All measurements include ¼"-wide seam allowances.
Cut all strips across the fabric width (crosswise grain).

From each of the 16 plaid, checked, and striped fabrics, cut:

1 strip, 6½" wide, for a total of 16 strips. Cut 4 squares from each strip, each 6½" x 6½", for a total of 64 squares.

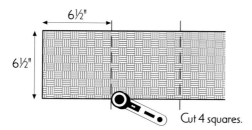

From the rust fabric, cut:

4 strips, each 2" wide; crosscut into 80 squares, each 2" x 2"

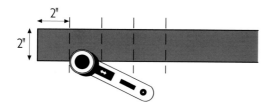

From each of the light and dark blue fabrics, cut:

1 strip, 2" wide; crosscut each strip into 16 squares, each 2" x 2", for a total of 32 squares

From the medium blue fabric, cut:

3 strips, each 2" wide; crosscut into 48 squares, each 2" x 2"

From each of the navy blue, yellow-brown, and gold fabrics, cut:

2 strips, each 2" wide. Crosscut strips into 2" x 2" squares. You need 32 squares of each color.

PIECING
(by hand or machine)

Marie-Christine learned this easy piecing method in a workshop conducted by Mary Ellen Hopkins.

1. Draw a diagonal line from corner to corner on the wrong side of each small square (B).

2. Place 4 small squares (B) of the same color on a large square (A) with right sides together. Pin in place.

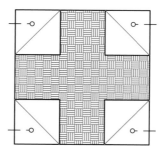

3. Hand or machine stitch on the diagonal line of each small square.

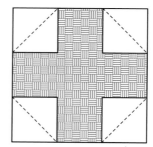

N O T E

If you sew by hand, it is absolutely necessary for this piecing to begin and end at the outer edges of the square, rather than ending at the seam intersections as is normally done when hand piecing.

4. Cut away a small triangle of the small square only, leaving a seam allowance beyond the stitching. The background square behind adds stability to the corners of the finished block.

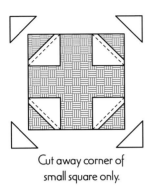

Cut away corner of small square only.

5. Fold the remainder of each small square to the corner of the large square and finger-press.

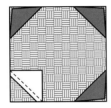

6. Repeat with the remaining small and large squares to make a total of 64 blocks.

7. Press each block carefully, making sure that all corners are square.

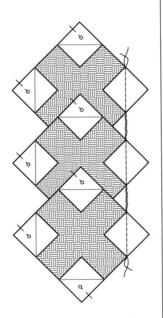

If you machine piece, prepare all the blocks as described in step 2. Then chain piece by feeding the blocks into the presser foot, one after the other, without breaking the stitching between blocks. After sewing a square to one corner of each block, remove the "chain" from the machine, snip the thread chains between the blocks, and chain sew the next set of corners.

QUILT TOP ASSEMBLY AND FINISHING

1. Arrange the blocks in 8 rows of 8 blocks each. (Refer to the quilt plan on page 75 and the photo on page 76 for color placement or arrange as desired.)

2. Join the blocks in horizontal rows and press the seams in opposite directions from row to row as indicated by the arrows in the illustration below.

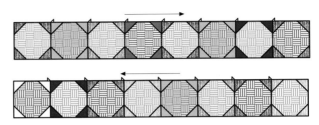

3. Sew the rows together.
4. Lightly press the completed quilt top.
5. Mark quilting lines across both diagonals of the blocks.

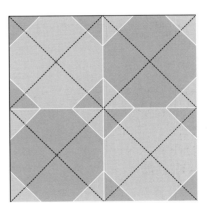

6. Layer the quilt top with batting and backing; baste. (See pages 24–25.)

7. Quilt on the marked line.

8. Cut two 1¼"-wide strips each from 4 of the leftover solid fabrics. Join each set as shown on page 28 to make 4 binding strips. Press seams open.

9. Bind each quilt edge, following the "Method One" directions on pages 28–29 for attaching binding.

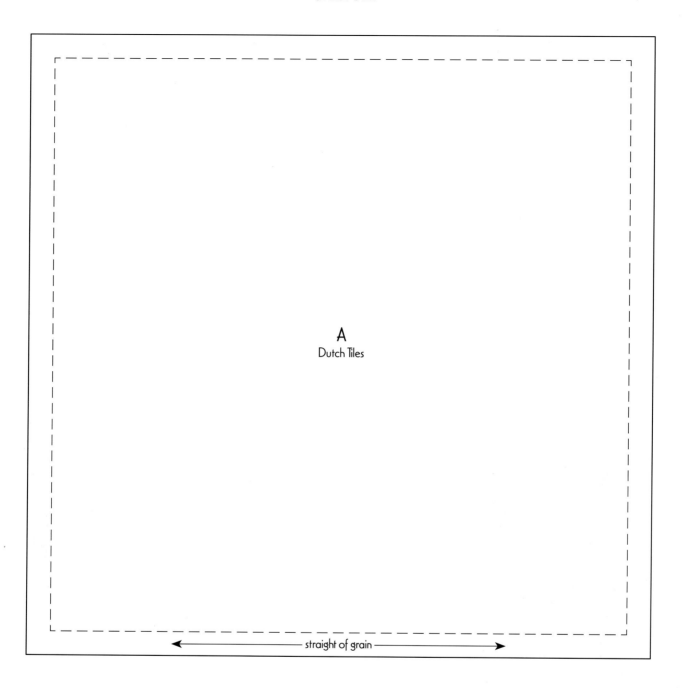

A
Dutch Tiles

straight of grain

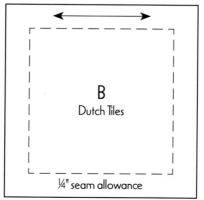

B
Dutch Tiles

¼" seam allowance

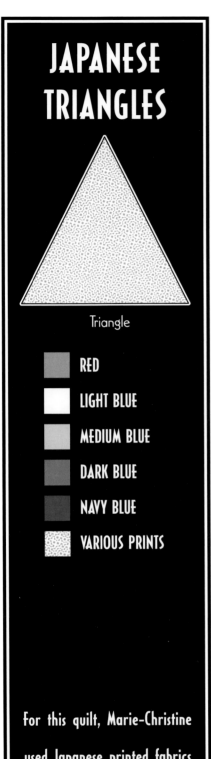

JAPANESE TRIANGLES

Triangle

RED

LIGHT BLUE

MEDIUM BLUE

DARK BLUE

NAVY BLUE

VARIOUS PRINTS

For this quilt, Marie-Christine used Japanese printed fabrics (Yukata cloth) with solid fabrics. Create a similar effect by using six printed fabrics with Japanese motifs.

Quilt Size: 26½" x 38½"
Finished Size of Triangles: 4" high with a 4" base

MATERIALS
44"-wide fabric

¾ yd. navy blue for the triangles, inner border, and binding
½ yd. red for the triangles and outer border
¼ yd. light blue for the triangles
¼ yd. medium blue for the triangles
¼ yd. dark blue for the triangles
⅓ yd. each of 6 different prints for the triangles*
⅞ yd. for the backing
30" x 42" piece of batting

Japanese Yukata cloth generally measures about 15½" wide. If you prefer to use it, purchase ½-yard pieces of 6 different prints. Be sure to test for colorfastness as the blue dyes may bleed. See "Preparation" on page 7.

JAPANESE TRIANGLES

Japanese Triangles by Marie-Christine Flocard, les Loges en Josas, France, 1991. 26½" x 38½". Machine pieced and hand quilted.

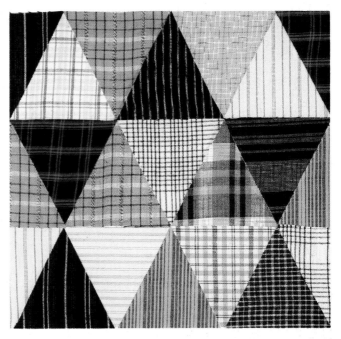

TEMPLATE CUTTING*

Use the templates on page 85. All templates and strip measurements include ¼"-wide seam allowances. Cut all strips across the fabric width (crosswise grain).

Due to the scrappy nature of this quilt, directions are for template cutting only.

From the navy blue, cut:

4 strips, each 2½" x 42", for the inner border

4 strips, each 1¼" x 42", for the binding

8 triangles (Template A)

2 half-triangles (Template B)

From the red, cut:

4 strips, each 1½" x 42", for the outer border

2 triangles (Template A)

4 half-triangles (Template B)

From the light blue, cut:

3 triangles (Template A)

From the medium blue, cut:

2 triangles (Template A)

From the dark blue, cut:

4 triangles (Template A)

From the prints cut:

a total of 53 triangles (Template A); cut 8 each from 3 different prints; 9 each from 2 different prints; and 11 from the remaining print

a total of 10 half-triangles (Template B); cut 2 each from five different prints

PIECING
(by hand or machine)

1. If you piece by machine, mark the seam intersections on the wrong side of each triangle and half-triangle, using a sharp pencil. If you piece by hand, the seam lines should already be marked on the wrong side of each triangle (A) and half-triangle (B).

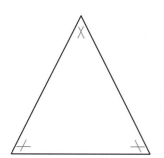

2. Arrange the triangles and half-triangles in 8 horizontal rows of 9 triangles each, placing a half-triangle at each end of each row. Refer to the quilt plan (page 81) and the color photo (page 82) for color placement.

3. To join the triangles and half-triangles in horizontal rows, pin neighboring pieces together, carefully matching seam intersections. Stitch.

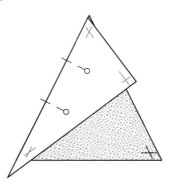

4. Press seams in opposite directions from row to row as shown.

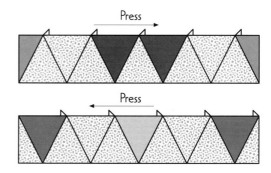

5. Sew the completed rows together.

6. Sew each 2½"-wide strip of navy blue fabric to a 1½"-wide red strip. Press the seam toward the navy blue strip in each strip unit.

Make 4.

7. Sew the borders to the quilt top as shown for "Borders with Mitered Corners" on pages 21–22.

FINISHING

1. Lightly press the completed quilt top.
2. Center and mark a 2½"-diameter circle over each junction where 6 triangles come together.

3. Layer the quilt top with batting and backing; baste. (See pages 24–25.)
4. Quilt on the marked lines, using white Sashiko thread.
5. Bind the edges of the quilt with navy blue, straight-grain binding, following the "Method Two" directions on pages 29–30 for attaching binding.

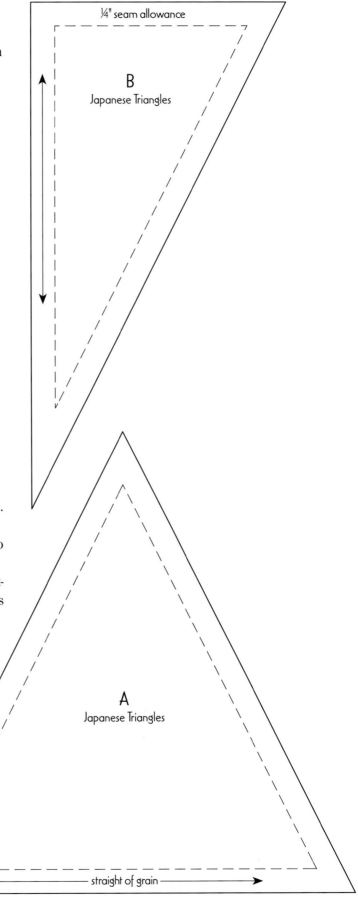

¼" seam allowance

B
Japanese Triangles

A
Japanese Triangles

straight of grain

CARD TRICK

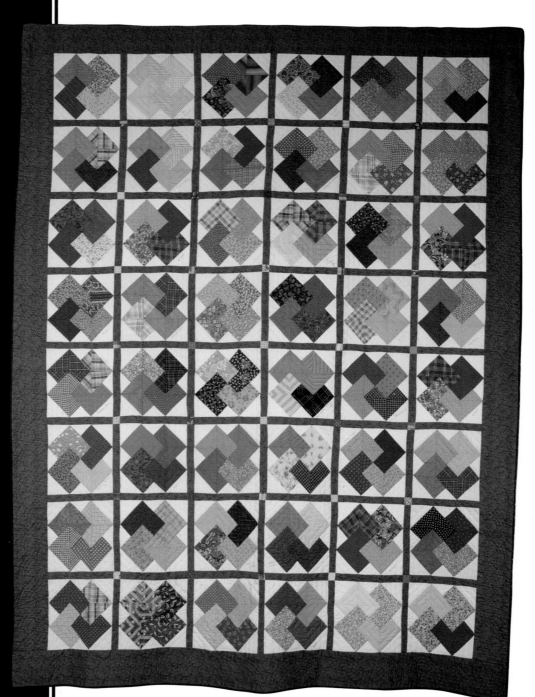

Card Trick, a friendship quilt pieced by hand and machine by the staff of Le Rouvray, Paris, France, 1990. 79¼" x 102¾". Hand quilted in 1994 by Marie-Jeanne Bourdier.

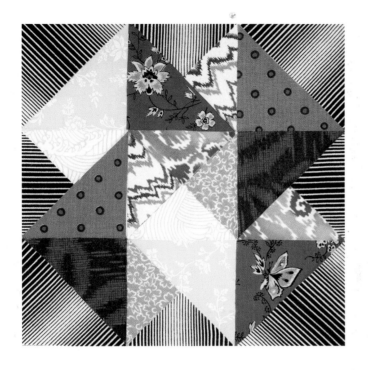

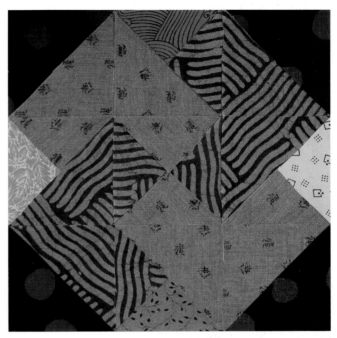

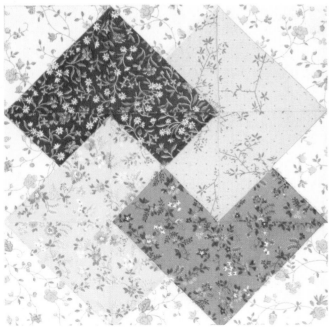

CARD TRICK

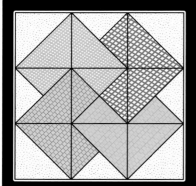

Card Trick Block

The Le Rouvray team pieced this friendship quilt and gave it to Marie-Jeanne Bourdier when she left Paris for Poitiers. Marie-Jeanne did the beautiful quilting. Each friend donated treasured fabrics for the patchwork. Use fabric from your scrap bag or buy eight different prints to create your own scrappy quilt.

  Quilt Size: 79¼" x 102¾"
Finished Block Size: 10½" x 10½"

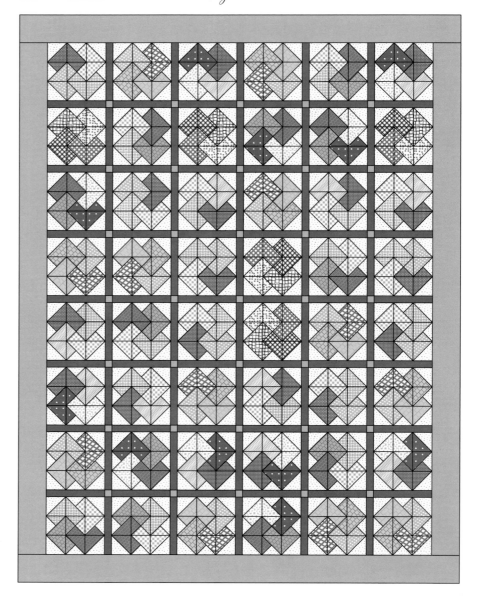

MATERIALS
44"-wide fabric
2½ yds. off-white solid for the block backgrounds

1 yd. each of 8 different prints for the cornerstones and blocks

3¼ yds. gray print for the sashing and borders

6 yds. for the backing

83" x 107" piece of batting

⅜ yd. solid gray for binding

TEMPLATE CUTTING
Use the templates on page 91. All templates and strip measurements include ¼"-wide seam allowances. Cut all strips across the fabric width (crosswise grain) unless otherwise directed.

From the off-white solid, cut:

192 triangles (Template A)

192 triangles (Template B)

From the 8 prints, cut:

A total of 35 assorted squares (Template C) for the sashing cornerstones

Next, choose 4 fabrics of different colors for 1 block. From each of these fabrics cut:

2 triangles (Template A), for a total of 8

2 triangles (Template B), for a total of 8

Repeat the above 47 times to cut enough pieces for 48 blocks.

From the gray print, cut:

2 strips, each 5¼" x 108", for the side borders; cut along the fabric length

2 strips, each 5¼" x 82", for the top and bottom borders; cut along the fabric length

82 strips, each 1¾" x 11", for the sashing

From the gray solid, cut:

9 strips, each 1¼" x 42", for the binding

ROTARY CUTTING

From the off-white solid, cut:

11 strips, each 4⅜" x 42"; crosscut into 96 squares, each 4⅜" x 4⅜". Cut each of the squares once diagonally for a total of 192 triangles.

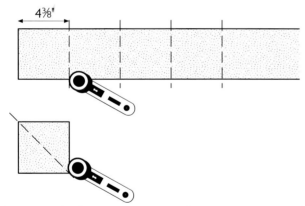

6 strips, each 4¾" x 42"; crosscut into 48 squares, each 4¾" x 4¾". Cut each of the squares twice diagonally for a total of 192 triangles.

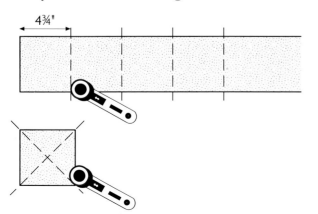

From each of the 8 prints, cut:

3 strips, each 4⅜" x 42"; crosscut into 24 squares, each 4⅜" x 4⅜". Cut each of the squares once diagonally for a total of 48 triangles of each color (384 triangles total).

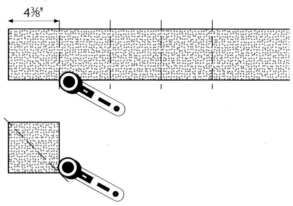

2 strips, each 4¾" x 42"; crosscut into 12 squares, each 4¾" x 4¾". Cut squares twice diagonally for a total of 48 triangles of each color (384 triangles total).

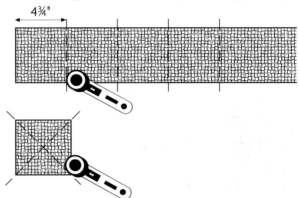

5 squares, each 1¾" x 1¾", for a total of 40 cornerstones for the sashing. You need only 35; set 5 aside for other patchwork projects.

From the gray print, cut:

2 strips, each 5¼" x 108", for the side borders; cut along the fabric length

2 strips, each 5¼" x 82", for the top and bottom borders; cut along the fabric length

10 strips, each 1¾" x 108"; cut along the fabric length; crosscut into 82 strips, each 1¾" x 11", for the sashing

From the gray solid cut:

9 strips, each 1¼" x 42", for the binding

PIECING
(by hand or machine)

Make each of the 48 blocks required in the following manner.

1. Lay out the pieces for one block, following the block diagram for color placement.

 Lay out the pieces for a few blocks at a time to speed your work.

2. For each block, sew the 4 large-triangle pairs (A) together on the long bias edges, taking care not to stretch them as you sew. Return the completed units to the block layout, paying careful attention to color placement.

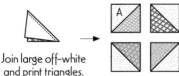

Join large off-white and print triangles.

3. Sew the 4 small-triangle pairs (B) together on the short edges. Sew each small-triangle unit to a large triangle (A). Return the completed units to the block layout, paying careful attention to color placement.

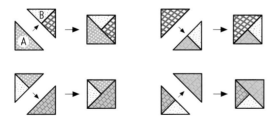

4. Sew the center small triangles (B) together in pairs, then pin the pairs together carefully so seams match at the center. Stitch to complete the center unit. Return to the block layout.

5. Sew the units together in horizontal rows, pressing the seams in opposite directions from row to row. Join the rows to complete each block. Make a total of 48 blocks.

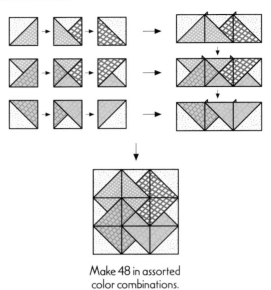

Make 48 in assorted color combinations.

6. Measure all blocks to make sure that they are 11" x 11". Adjust if necessary.

QUILT TOP ASSEMBLY

1. Arrange the blocks in 8 horizontal rows of 6 blocks each with five 1¾" x 11" sashing strips between them. Sew the rows of blocks and sashing together and press the seams toward the strips.

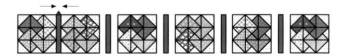

2. Make 7 long sashing strips, alternating six 1¾" x 11" gray strips, with the five 1¾" cornerstone squares (C). Sew the pieces together and press the seams toward the sashing strips.

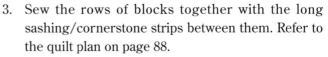

3. Sew the rows of blocks together with the long sashing/cornerstone strips between them. Refer to the quilt plan on page 88.

4. Attach gray borders to the quilt top as shown for "Borders with Straight-Cut Corners" on page 21.

FINISHING

1. Lightly press the completed quilt top.
2. Mark quilting as shown.

3. Cut the backing fabric into two pieces of equal length. Cut one of the 2 pieces in half lengthwise and sew the resulting strips to the long edges of the remaining piece of backing. Press the seams open.

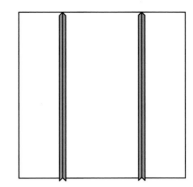

4. Layer the quilt top with batting and backing; baste. See "Layering the Quilt" on pages 24–25.
5. Quilt on the marked lines.
6. Sew the gray binding strips together, end to end, and press the seams open. Bind the quilt edges, following the "Method One" directions on pages 28–29 for attaching binding.

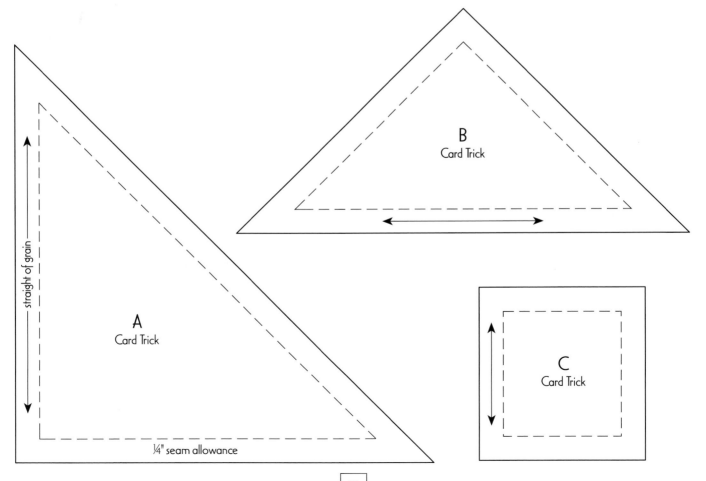

straight of grain

A
Card Trick

¼" seam allowance

B
Card Trick

C
Card Trick

WINDMILL

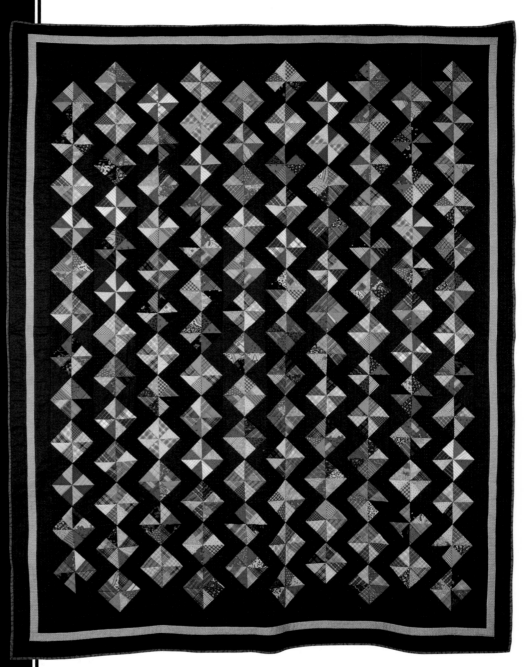

Windmill
by Willemke Vidinic,
Paris, France, 1993.
59½" x 74½".
Machine pieced
and machine quilted.

WINDMILL

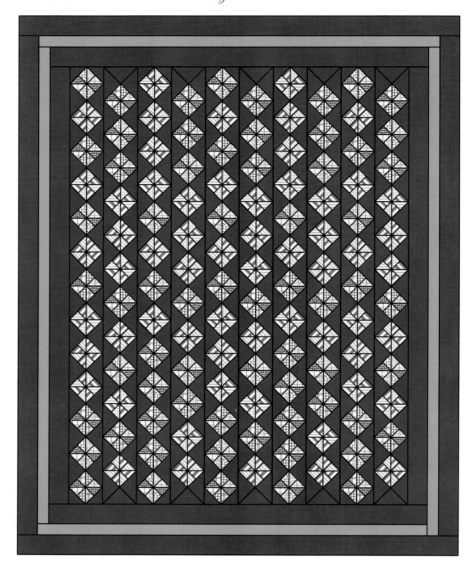

Windmill Block

Will made this quilt with a wide variety of scraps, including many checked fabrics. If you do not have a large scrap collection, achieve a scrappy look with the fabrics in the "Materials" list at right.

Quilt Size: 59½" x 74½"
Finished Block Size: 3½" x 3½"

MATERIALS
44"-wide fabric

½ yd. each of 8 different fabrics (prints, solids, and checks of your choice) for the blocks in light and dark values of red, yellow, beige, brown, and blue

3⅜ yds. navy blue for the setting and corner triangles

½ yd. light blue for the inner border

⅓ yd. red print for the binding

4⅛ yds. for the backing

63" x 78" piece of batting

TEMPLATE CUTTING

Use the templates on page 97. All templates and strip measurements include ¼"-wide seam allowances. Cut all strips across the fabric width (crosswise grain).

From each of the 8 different fabrics, cut:

125 Template C for a total of 1000 triangles for the blocks

From the navy blue, cut:

14 strips, each 2¼" x 42", for the inner and outer borders

20 Template B for corner setting triangles

260 Template A for side setting triangles. Arrange and trace the templates in the manner shown to make best use of the fabric.

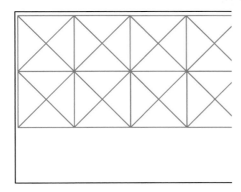

From the light blue, cut:

7 strips, each 1½" x 42", for the middle border

From the red print, cut:

8 strips, each 1¼" x 42", for the binding

ROTARY CUTTING

Cut all strips across the fabric width (crosswise grain).

From each of the 8 different fabrics for the blocks, cut:

5 strips, each 2⅝" x 42"; crosscut each set of strips into 63 squares, each 2⅝" x 2⅝". Cut the squares once diagonally for 126 triangles (C) of each fabric. You need a total of 1000 triangles. Set the extra triangle of each fabric aside for use in another project.

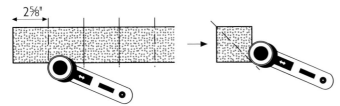

From the navy blue, cut:

14 strips, each 2¼" x 42", for the inner and outer borders

11 strips, each 6¼" x 6¼"; crosscut into 65 squares, each 6¼" x 6¼". Cut these squares twice diagonally for 260 side setting triangles (A).

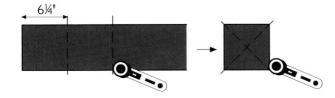

1 strip, 3⅜" x 42"; crosscut 10 squares, each 3⅜" x 3⅜". Cut these squares once diagonally for 20 corner setting triangles (B).

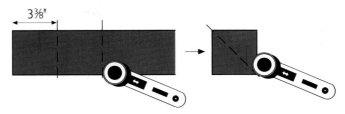

From the light blue, cut:

7 strips, each 1½" x 42", for the middle border

From the red print, cut:

8 strips, each 1¼" x 42", for the binding

PIECING

(by hand or machine)

Make 125 blocks following the directions below. If you machine piece, we recommend using chain piecing, shown on page 19, to speed your work.

1. For each block, arrange 8 triangles as shown.

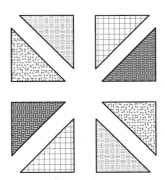

 There are several ways to arrange the triangles for the blocks.

☐ *Use triangles of only two different fabrics in each block.*

☐ *Use four colors, each in a light and dark value. Alternate the dark and light triangles in each block.*

☐ *Arrange the triangles randomly, using more than four colors in a block. This was the option chosen for the quilt shown on page 92.*

2. Sew triangle pairs together along the long, bias edge. Be careful not to stretch the edge as you stitch. Plan

the pressing so that all seams face the same direction as you position them in the block.

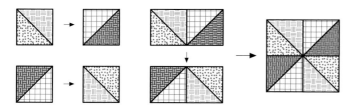

3. Sew the triangle pairs together as shown to complete the block.

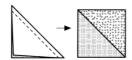

4. Arrange the completed blocks in rows as shown in the quilt plan on page 94, adding navy blue side setting triangles (A) and corner setting triangles (B) as indicated. For each odd-numbered row, you need 13 blocks, 24 triangles (A), and 4 triangles (B). For each even-numbered row, you need 12 blocks and 28 triangles (A).

5. Sew the pieces together in diagonal rows, then join the rows to complete each strip of blocks. In odd-numbered rows, add the corner setting triangles to each end last.

Rows 1, 3, 5, 7, 9   Rows 2, 4, 6, 8, 10

QUILT TOP ASSEMBLY

1. Sew the completed strips of blocks and triangles together, being sure to alternate the two types (odd and even rows) as shown in the quilt plan. Press the seams toward the even-numbered rows.

2. Sew 6 navy blue strips together, end to end, and press the seams open.

3. Measure the quilt top as shown for "Borders with Straight-Cut Corners" on page 21. Cut and sew the navy blue inner borders to the long edges of the quilt, then measure, cut, and sew the inner borders to the top and bottom edges.

4. Repeat with the light blue strips for the middle border and then with the remaining navy blue strips for the outer border. Sew borders to the long sides of the quilt first, then to the top and bottom edges.

FINISHING

1. Lightly press the completed quilt top.
2. Mark quilting lines as desired or plan to quilt the pieced squares in-the-ditch as in the quilt in the photo.

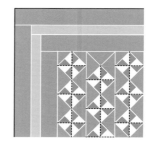

3. Cut the backing fabric into 2 pieces of equal length. Cut 2 long strips, each 12" wide, from one of the pieces. Sew these to the long edges of the other piece of backing. Press the seams open.

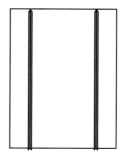

4. Layer the quilt top with batting and backing; baste.
5. Quilt on the marked lines or as desired.
6. Attach the red-print binding strips to the quilt, using the binding method of your choice. See "Adding Binding" on pages 28–30.

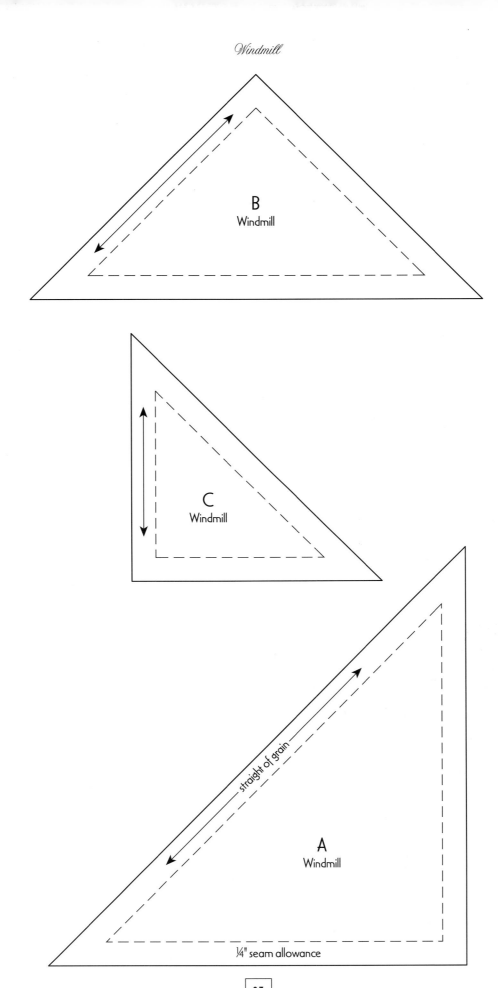

B
Windmill

C
Windmill

straight of grain

A
Windmill

¼" seam allowance

MOSAICS

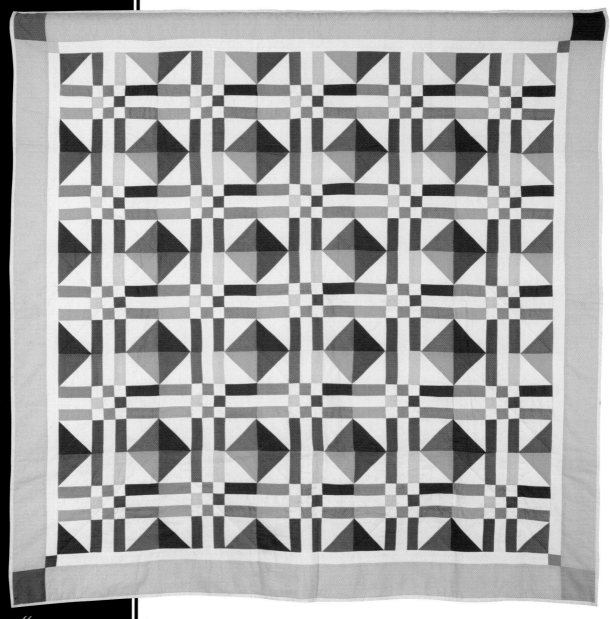

Mosaics
by Cosabeth Parriaud,
Paris, France, 1990.
52½" x 52½".
Machine pieced and
hand quilted.

MOSAICS

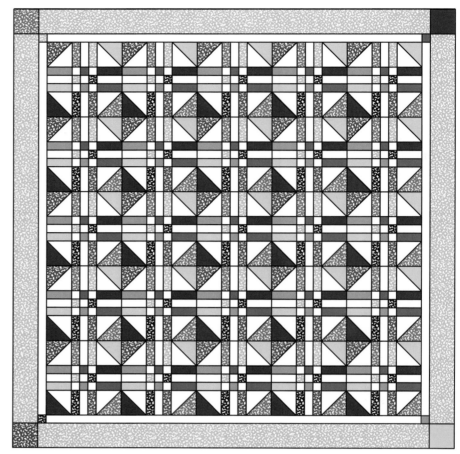

Mosaic Block

■	OFF-WHITE
▓	LIGHT GREEN (C-1)
▓	DARK GREEN (C-2)
▓	MUSTARD YELLOW (C-3)
▓	YELLOW-BROWN (C-4)
■	DARK BLUE-GREEN (C-5)
▓	LIGHT BLUE-GREEN (C-6)
▓	DUSTY ROSE (C-7)
▓	MAUVE (C-8)

The block in this quilt fools the eye because of the way color is used. Each color has a color number to make assembly easier.

Quilt Size: 52½ " x 52½ "
Finished Block Size: 9 " x 9 "

MATERIALS
44"-wide fabric

2¼ yds. off-white for the inner
   border and blocks
1⅛ yds. light green (C1)
⅝ yd. dark green (C2)
⅝ yd. mustard yellow (C3)
⅜ yd. yellow-brown (C4)
⅝ yd. dark blue-green (C5)
⅜ yd. light blue-green (C6)
⅝ yd. dusty rose (C7)
⅜ yd. mauve (C8)
3¼ yds. for the backing
57" x 57" piece of batting
⅓ yd. off-white for the binding

NOTE
*Due to the number
of pieces required for each
block, we recommend rotary
cutting and machine piecing.
However, we also include
instructions and templates
for traditional piecing.*

TEMPLATE CUTTING

Use the templates on page 105. All templates and strip measurements include ¼"-wide seam allowances. Cut all strips across the fabric width (crosswise grain).

From the off-white for the inner border and blocks, cut:

8 strips, each 1½" x 42", for the inner border

100 triangles (Template A) for the blocks

100 rectangles (Template B) for the blocks

125 squares (Template C) for the blocks

From the light green (C-1), cut:

8 strips, each 3" x 42", for the outer borders

25 rectangles (Template B) for the blocks

26 squares (Template C) for the blocks and 1 inner-border cornerstone

From the dark green (C-2), cut:

25 triangles (Template A) for the blocks

25 rectangles (Template B) for the blocks

1 square (Template D) for an outer-border cornerstone

From the mustard yellow (C-3), cut:

25 triangles (Template A) for the blocks

25 rectangles (Template B) for the blocks

1 square (Template D), for an outer-border cornerstone

From the yellow-brown (C-4), cut:

25 rectangles (Template B) for the blocks

26 squares (Template C) for the blocks and one inner-border cornerstone

From the dark blue-green (C-5), cut:

25 triangles (Template A) for the blocks

25 rectangles (Template B) for the blocks

1 square (Template D) for an outer-border cornerstone

From the light blue-green (C-6), cut:

25 rectangles (Template B) for the blocks

26 squares (Template C) for the blocks and one inner-border cornerstone

From the dusty rose (C-7), cut:

25 triangles (Template A) for the blocks

25 rectangles (Template B) for the blocks

1 square (Template D) for an outer-border cornerstone

From the mauve (C-8), cut:

25 rectangles (Template B) for the blocks

26 squares (Template C) for the blocks and one inner-border cornerstone

From the off-white fabric for the binding, cut:

6 strips, each 1¼" x 42"

ROTARY CUTTING

Cut all strips across the fabric width (crosswise grain). All strip measurements include ¼"-wide seam allowances.

From the off-white for the inner border and blocks, cut:

25 strips, each 1½" x 42". Set aside 8 strips for the inner border and use the remainder for the blocks.

4 rectangles, each 10" x 30", for the blocks

From the light green (C-1), cut:

8 strips, each 3" x 42", for the outer borders

4 strips, each 1½" x 42", for the blocks

1 square, 1½" x 1½", for an inner-border cornerstone (C)

From the dark green (C-2), cut:

3 strips, each 1½" x 42", for the blocks

1 rectangle, 10" x 30", for the blocks

1 square, 3" x 3", for an outer-border cornerstone (D)

From the mustard yellow (C-3), cut:

3 strips, each 1½" x 42", for the blocks

1 rectangle, 10" x 30", for the blocks

1 square, 3" x 3", for an outer-border cornerstone (D)

From the yellow-brown (C-4), cut:

4 strips, each 1½" x 42", for the blocks

1 square, 1½" x 1½", for an inner-border cornerstone (C)

From the dark blue-green (C-5), cut:

3 strips, each 1½" x 42", for the blocks

1 rectangle, 10" x 30", for the blocks

1 square, 3" x 3", for an outer-border cornerstone (D)

From the light blue-green (C-6), cut:

4 strips, each 1½" x 42", for the blocks

1 square, 1½" x 1½", for an inner-border cornerstone (C)

From the dusty rose (C-7), cut:

3 strips, each 1½" x 42", for the blocks

1 rectangle, 10" x 30", for the blocks

1 square, 3" x 3", for an outer-border cornerstone (D)

From the mauve (C-8), cut:

4 strips, each 1½" x 42", for the blocks

1 square, 1½" x 1½", for an inner-border cornerstone (C)

From the off-white for the binding, cut:

6 strips, each 1¼" x 42"

TRADITIONAL PIECING

1. Sew rectangles (B) together in the following combinations to make a total of 100 Unit 1. Press all seams away from the off-white pieces.

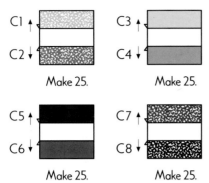

C1 ↑
C2 ↓
Make 25.

C3 ↑
C4 ↓
Make 25.

C5 ↑
C6 ↓
Make 25.

C7 ↑
C8 ↓
Make 25.

2. Sew squares (C) together to make 25 Unit 2.

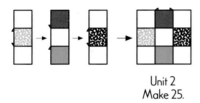

Unit 2
Make 25.

3. Join triangles (A) for a total of 100 Unit 3.

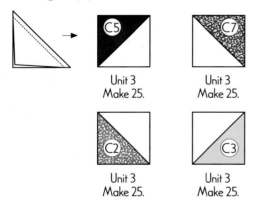

Unit 3
Make 25.

Unit 3
Make 25.

Unit 3
Make 25.

Unit 3
Make 25.

4. Complete the quilt, following the directions for "Quilt Top Assembly" on page 104.

MACHINE SPEED PIECING

Unit 1

1. Sew strips, right sides together and raw edges matching, into the strip-pieced units shown above right; make 3 units of each color combination. Press all seams away from the off-white strips as indicated by the arrows.

2. Cut 25 squares, each 3½" x 3½", from each strip-pieced color combination. Set leftover strip units aside for other projects. You need a total of 100 Unit 1 (25 of each color).

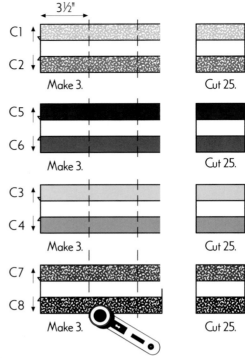

3½"

C1 ↑
C2 ↓
Make 3.   Cut 25.

C5 ↑
C6 ↓
Make 3.   Cut 25.

C3 ↑
C4 ↓
Make 3.   Cut 25.

C7 ↑
C8 ↓
Make 3.   Cut 25.

Unit 2

1. With right sides together and long raw edges matching, sew strips into the strip-pieced units shown below. Press the seams away from the off-white strips as shown by the arrows in the diagram. Cut the strip-pieced units into 1½"-wide segments.

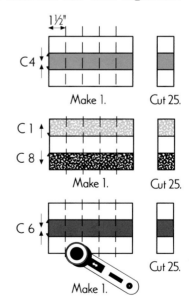

1½"

C4 ↕
Make 1.   Cut 25.

C1 ↑
C8 ↓
Make 1.   Cut 25.

C6 ↕
Make 1.   Cut 25.

2. Sew the segments together as shown.

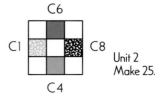

C6

C1   C8

Unit 2
Make 25.

C4

Unit 3

1. On the wrong side of each 10" x 30" off-white rectangle, draw a grid with 13 squares, each 3⅞" x 3⅞". Draw diagonal lines through each square.

2. Place each off-white rectangle on top of a solid-color rectangle with right sides together and raw edges matching. Pin the layers together. Stitch ¼" from each side of the diagonal lines.

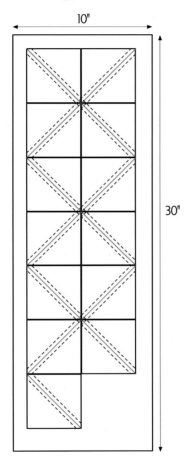

10"

30"

3. Place the stitched rectangles on the rotary-cutting mat and cut along the vertical and horizontal lines. You will get 13 squares from each set of fabrics.

Cut 13.

4. Cut each resulting square diagonally between the two rows of stitching. You need a total of 26 triangle pairs from each set of fabrics.

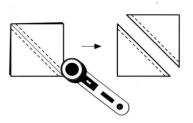

5. Press the seam in each pair toward the darker color, working carefully to avoid stretching the bias seam. You will have a total of 104 half-square triangle units. You need 25 of each color combination. Set aside the extra unit of each color for another project.

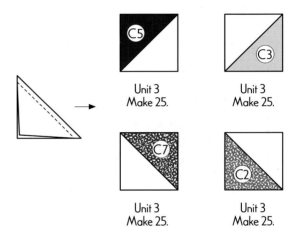

C5

Unit 3
Make 25.

C3

Unit 3
Make 25.

C7

Unit 3
Make 25.

C2

Unit 3
Make 25.

BLOCK ASSEMBLY

1. Referring to the block diagram for color placement, arrange the completed units into 25 identical blocks.

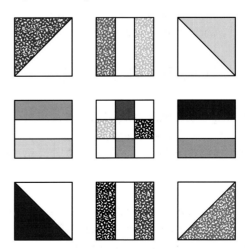

2. Pin the units together for stitching, making sure that all seam lines match precisely. Join the units in vertical rows and press the seams away from the off-white pieces as indicated by the arrows.

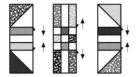

3. Pin and sew the vertical rows together to complete each block. Pin carefully so that all seam lines match precisely.

QUILT TOP ASSEMBLY

1. Referring to the quilt plan on page 100 and the color photo on page 98, arrange the blocks in 5 rows of 5 blocks each. Sew the blocks together in rows, pressing the seams in opposite directions from row to row.

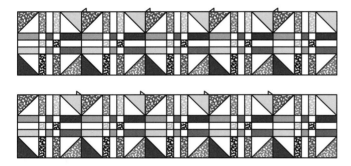

2. Sew the rows together.

3. Sew the off-white inner border strips together in pairs as shown to make 4 long strips. Press the seams open. Repeat with the light green strips.

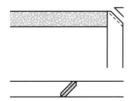

4. Measure the quilt top through the center as shown on page 21 and cut 4 off-white 1½"-wide strips to match that measurement. Sew a border to the top and bottom edges of the quilt top as shown on page 21 for "Borders with Straight-Cut Corners." Press the seam toward the quilt top.

5. Sew a 1½" square (C) to each end of each remaining off-white border strip, referring to the illustration for color placement. Press the seams toward the squares. Sew the borders to the sides of the quilt top.

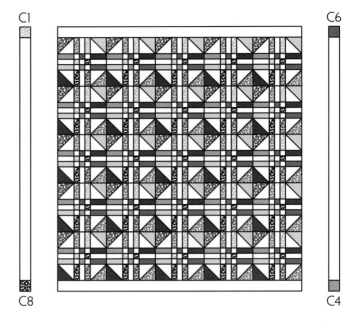

6. Repeat steps 4 and 5 above, using the light green border strips and the 3" squares (D).

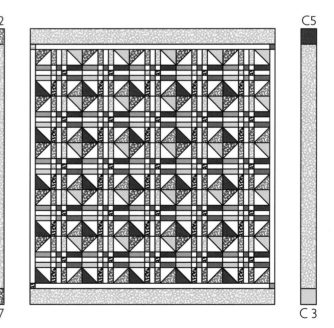

FINISHING

1. Lightly press the completed quilt top.
2. Mark quilting lines across the diagonals of each block. Add more lines if desired.

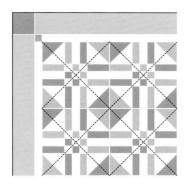

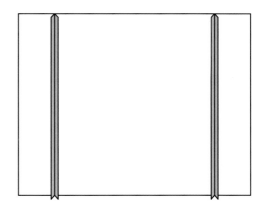

3. Cut the backing fabric into two pieces of equal length. From one of the pieces, cut 2 strips, each 9" wide. Sew to the long edges of the other backing piece. Press the seams open.

4. Layer the quilt top with batting and backing; baste.
5. Quilt on the marked lines.
6. Sew the off-white binding strips together, end to end, and press the seams open. Bind the quilt edges, following the "Method Two" directions on pages 29–30 for attaching binding.

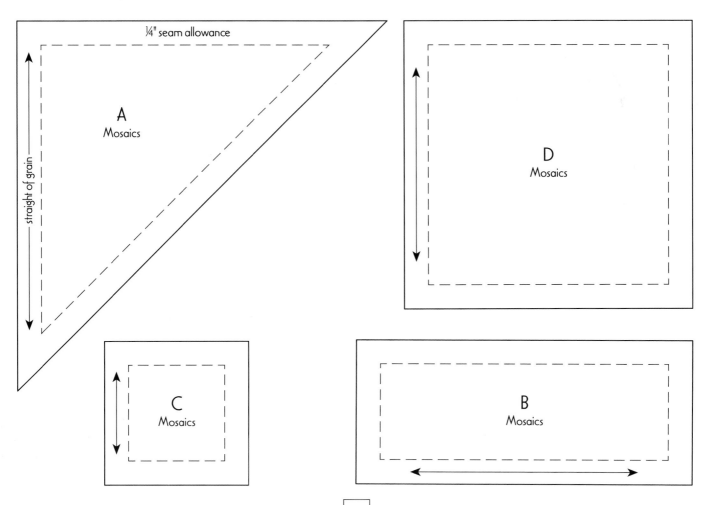

LITTLE STARS

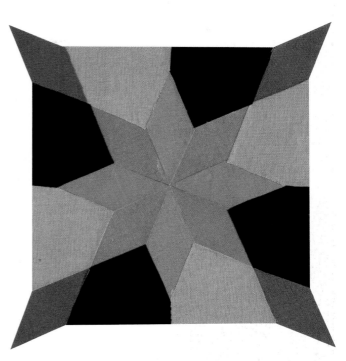

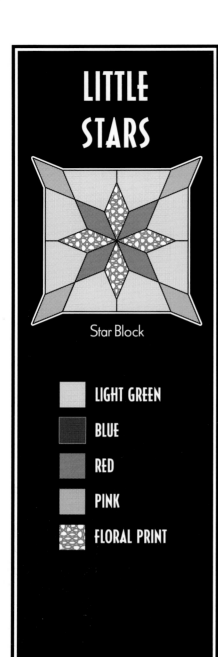

LITTLE STARS

Star Block

■	LIGHT GREEN
■	BLUE
■	RED
■	PINK
▦	FLORAL PRINT

Colorful stars made of diamonds were set into green background blocks to create this design. Try this one after you have made one or more of the easier quilts in this book.

Quilt Size: 43" x 54"
Finished Block Size: 14¾" diagonal (approximate)

MATERIALS
44"-wide fabric

1¾ yds. light green solid for the alternate blocks and the block background
⅜ yd. blue solid for the diamonds
⅜ yd. red solid for the diamonds
⅜ yd. pink solid for the joining diamonds at the block corners

⅝ yd. coordinating print for blocks
3⅜ yds. for the backing*
47" x 58" piece of batting
¾ yd. total of assorted floral prints for binding

You only need 1¾ yards for the backing if the fabric is at least 45" wide after preshrinking.

TEMPLATE CUTTING*

Use the templates on page 111. All seam allowances are ¼" wide.

Due to the unusual shapes, we do not give rotary-cutting directions. *Cut the light green background squares with a rotary cutter if you prefer.*

From the light green, cut:

20 squares, each 7¼" x 7¼", for the alternate blocks

80 Template B and 80 Template B reversed

From the blue, cut:

49 diamonds (Template A)

From the red, cut:

49 diamonds (Template A)

From the pink, cut:

49 diamonds (Template A)

From the coordinating print, cut:

80 diamonds (Template A)

From the assorted floral prints, cut:

enough 1¼"-wide bias strips to total 7 yds

HAND PIECING

We recommend piecing this quilt by hand because the unusually shaped blocks require many inset seams. Before you start sewing, mark the seam lines on the wrong side of each piece, using a sharp pencil and a ruler. If you plan to machine piece, it is only necessary to make crosshair marks at the seam intersections as shown.

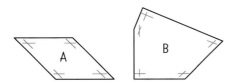

Star Blocks

Follow the directions below to prepare 6 blue-and-print and 6 red-and-print Star blocks:

1. For each blue star, sew a blue diamond (A) to a print diamond (A), sewing from seam intersection to seam intersection, *not raw edge to raw edge.* Stitch all the pieces in this manner, whether sewing by hand or machine. Press the seam toward the blue diamond. Make 4 diamond pairs for each of the 6 blue blocks. Repeat with red diamonds and print diamonds, pressing the seams toward the red diamonds.

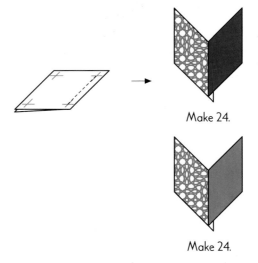

Make 24.

Make 24.

2. Join 2 matching pairs to make half diamonds, always pressing seams in the same direction around the star halves.

Arrows indicate direction to press seams.

3. Join the half diamonds to complete the star, making sure that all points meet precisely in the center. Stitch from the center out to one edge. Check stitching to make sure that seams match at the center. Adjust if necessary, then stitch the second half of the seam from the center out. Press. A rose-like flower will form in the center on the wrong side of the completed star.

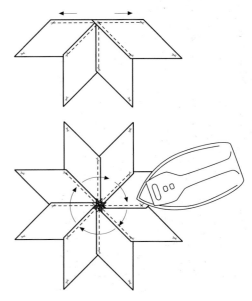

4. Add 4 light green Pieces B and 4 light green Pieces Br to each star, stitching in the direction of the arrows. Complete each star by stitching the Piece B edges together as shown.

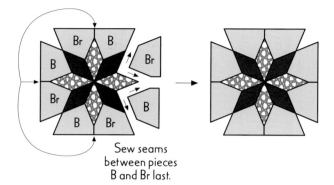

Sew seams between pieces B and Br last.

5. *Add a pink diamond to 2 corners only* of each block as shown, stitching in the direction of the arrows.

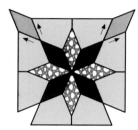

Star Block

Half-Blocks

Make 7 blue half-blocks and 7 red half-blocks.

1. For each half-block, sew 3 solid diamonds and 2 print diamonds together, as shown for the Star blocks.

2. Add 2 light green Pieces B and 2 Pieces B reversed to each of the 7 half-blocks as shown for the Star blocks. Sew the remaining seam between each pair of Piece B.

Sew short seams last.

Half-Block

3. Add a pink diamond to 3 of the blue half-blocks and 4 of the red half-blocks. See illustration above right.

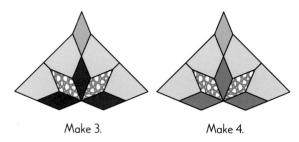

Make 3.   Make 4.

Corner Blocks

Make 2 red and 2 blue Corner blocks.

1. Sew 3 diamonds together for each Corner block.

2. Add 1 green Piece B and 1 Piece B reversed between the diamonds in each block. Sew the remaining edges of the 2 B pieces together.

Corner Block

QUILT TOP ASSEMBLY

1. Sew a Corner block to the top edge of a green square. Sew half-blocks to each side. Add the pink diamonds to the outer edges as shown below. Make 2 units.

2. Arrange the corner units from step 1 with the light green squares, Star blocks, half-blocks, and the remaining Corner blocks in diagonal rows as shown. Pay careful attention to the color placement so that the Star blocks and half-blocks create alternating diagonal rows of red and of blue. See illustration at the top of page 111.

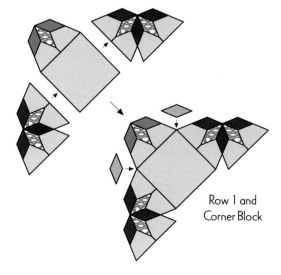

Row 1 and Corner Block

3. Sew the pieces together in each of the remaining diagonal rows.

4. Join the rows, setting the diamond points into the row above, as you did when sewing the diamonds to the block pieces.
5. Add the remaining pink diamonds around the outer edge, inserting them between the diamond points of the half-blocks. Refer to the quilt plan for placement.

FINISHING

1. Lightly press the completed quilt top.
2. Mark a wreath motif in the green background squares for quilting.

3. Cut the backing fabric into two pieces of equal length. Cut 2 strips, each 10" wide, from the length of 1 of the pieces. Sew 1 strip to each long edge of the remaining piece of backing.

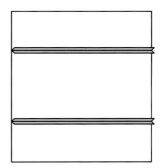

4. Layer the quilt top with batting and backing; baste.
5. Quilt on the marked lines in the green squares and stitch ⅛" to ¼" away from the seam lines in each diamond.
6. Join the assorted floral binding strips, end to end, to make a continuous strip of binding. Press the seams open. Bind the quilt edges, following the "Method One" directions on pages 28–29 for attaching binding. Miter the outer points and the inside corners of the irregular quilt edge.

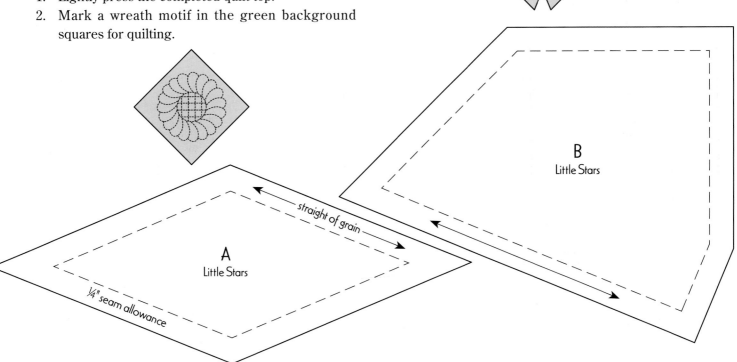

A
Little Stars

¼" seam allowance

straight of grain

B
Little Stars

That Patchwork Place Publications and Products